THE LANGUAGE OF
OIL&GAS

MICHAEL OWHOKO

Archway Publishing books may be ordered through booksellers or by contacting:

Archway Publishing
1663 Liberty Drive
Bloomington, IN 47403
www.archwaypublishing.com
1 (888) 242-5904

ISBN: 978-1-4808-9085-5 (sc)
ISBN: 978-1-4808-9086-2 (e)

Library of Congress Control Number: 2020908505

Print information available on the last page.

Archway Publishing rev. date: 5/12/2020

CONTENTS

PREFACE

One of the greatest challenges faced by energy journalists who report the oil and gas industry worldwide is knowledge of the language of the industry, and the concomitant capacity to communicate events succinctly and clearly to operators, experts and the general public without ambiguity.

The challenge is induced mainly by the fact that over 90 per cent of journalists who report the industry are non- science and engineering graduates. As a result, it has become increasingly imperative to put a reference material in place that will address this critical area of communication.

As an energy journalist in Nigeria, and one time Energy Editor, *Business Times;* Editor, *Nigerian Gas*; as well as Publicity Secretary, *Nigerian Gas Association*; and whose experience span over 20 years in the oil and gas industry, I know as a matter of fact that a book of this nature will facilitate the reportorial capacity of journalists assigned to Energy Beat.

This is why the idea of this book was first conceived in 1999, and when finishing touches were being put in place for its publication in 2007, the laptop containing the original manuscript was stolen. Subsequent attempts were also frustrated by unanticipated hiccups, making it impossible to publish the book at the projected time.

Perhaps, the absence of a reference material that is easily

accessible to journalists may have informed the popular newsroom maxim that if you want to expose the inefficiency of a journalist, particularly, a greenhorn, post him to the Energy Desk. This book will, no doubt, overwhelm these fears.

Besides the journalists, students, investors, contractors and businessmen who are venturing into the oil and gas turf for business opportunities will also find this book useful.

Care has been taken to comprehensively incorporate terminologies and expressions that are generally used in the oil and gas industry in this book. While it is true that specific term may vary slightly, extensive research has been made to ensure a balance.

INTRODUCTION

Every trade or profession has its language. The language is what gives it a unique identification, which also sets it apart from others. To be familiar with a trade or profession is to be acquainted with its language. Just like socio-cultural society that is characterised by linguistic setting, understanding a particular language, reinforces the capacity of integration into such society.

The oil and gas industry, just like other trade and professions, has its peculiar language. For those whose activities revolve round this industry, the surest way to build a bridge into it is to be familiar with its language. Not every stakeholder is a professional in this industry. Therefore, the target of this book is not the core professionals who have acquired knowledge of this business through formal studies in tertiary institutions, but the non-professionals. However, this does not completely erode the value and usefulness of this book to the professionals.

Other stakeholders are also critical to the overall success of the oil and gas business by virtue of their activities which have direct or indirect linkage to the industry. To be able to integrate into this industry, familiarity with the language and basic terms is imperative. Thus, this book serves as a dictionary of the oil and gas industry through which the meaning of technical lexicons as used in the industry are clearly explained and brought to the understanding of all stakeholders, including businessmen, contractors, practitioners, journalists and students.

The oil and gas industry is too important a sector for its language to be ignored. It is a sector that empowers other industries to drive their operations. Indeed, it is a catalyst for economy of the world. In reality, what can you do without the application of petroleum products as liquid of operation? From Manufacturing to Aviation to Medicals to Agriculture, and to other critical sectors, the role of petroleum products cannot be discounted.

Perhaps, no wonder the world is making frantic efforts in search of alternative to petroleum products in order to spread the risk of total dependency in case of eventuality. So far, the search continues for contingency. Notwithstanding the breakthrough on electricity and solar, they are still remote from posing any formidable threat of displacement to petroleum products.

The fact that the oil and gas industry is a multi-billion dollar project underscores the importance of having a clear understanding of its language. Thus, this book is a guide and a compass for stakeholders who have been doing business as well as those venturing into this turf anew.

Indeed, the book is a collector's choice, and is recommended to all who place premium on petroleum products.

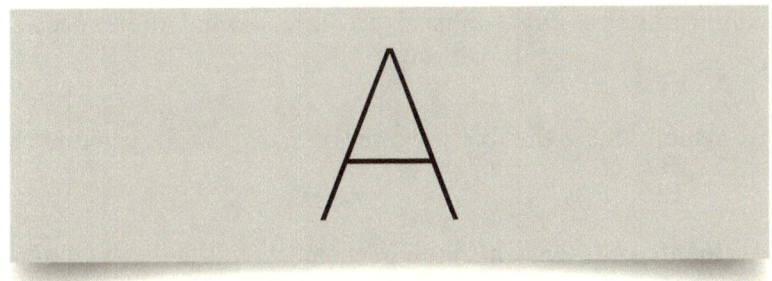

Abandonment. The dismantling of wellhead, production and transportation facilities due to cessation of utility by a company. It is the closing down of such a facility resulting in the discontinuation of its usage and termination of deliveries.

Abandoned Well. An oil well that has been put out of use due to unproductivity, inoperable condition or dryness, prompting the initial operators to deliberately relinquished their interests in the well. Abandoned wells are usually plugged to forestall seepage of oil, gas, or water from one formation to another.

Abatement. The process of curbing the intensity of pollution to reduce its impact. There are various applicable methods for doing this.

Abiotic Theory. A theory of the genesis of hydrocarbon which links the origin of a substantial portion of the earth's natural gas to inorganic processes. In other words, methane is believed to have been one of the earth's primeval gases, which predated the commencement of life and which remained trapped (and unoxidized) within the earth as the crust cooled.

Abnormal Pressure. Unusual pressure beyond the expected range.

Abrasion. This is the wearing away of machinery or pipeline by friction.

Accident. Any event which results in injury, and/or damage, and/or loss.

Aeration. This is the process of introducing air or gas into a liquid.

Account Classification. The categorization of customers by suppliers of natural gas or fuel oil for ease of billing. Customers are generally classified into "Industrial", "Commercial" and "Residential" for this purpose.

Accumulation. This refers to the quantity of oil and gas discovered in a reservoir rock in an oil field.

Acidizing. This is a process where hydrochloric acid is discharged into a reservoir to dissolve calcite aimed at causing increased flow from the reservoir.

Acid Rain. This relates to precipitation that has become acidic as a result of emission of sulfur oxides from fossil fuel burning power plants. It is rain mixed with sulfuric, nitric and other acids arising from emissions released during the burning of fossil fuels. Though not scientifically proven, it is believed that sulfuric and nitric acids in the atmosphere from man-made and natural emissions cause acid rain. Acid rain is a threat to ecosystems.

Acid Sludge. This is a black substance containing used acid and impurities resulting from petroleum oil treatment with sulfuric acid.

Acid Stimulation. Form of hydrochloric acid is pumped down well hole to enlarge pore space in oil bearing rocks to increase flow and recovery.

Acid Treating. This is a refining process in which sulfuric acid is applied to unfinished petroleum products like kerosene, gasoline and lubricating oil stocks to improve their colour, odour and other properties.

Acoustic Log. Record of time taken by a sound wave to travel over a certain distance through geological formations.

Acreage. A land area measured in acres and which is owned or controlled by person or persons with part or total shares of working interests.

Active Well. An oil well in good mechanical condition suitable for production or service use.

Actuals. The specific quantity of gas conveyed by a transporter on behalf of a shipper for which the latter is billed by the former.

Additives. These are blended chemicals in small volumes which are added to petroleum fuels, lubricants and other products to enhance their efficient and economic performance in engines and other equipment. Dyes, stabilizers, detergents, emulsifier, dispersant, antirust and antifreeze are other forms of additives used in gasoline. For example, dyes are used for grade identification, stabilizers for inhibiting oxidation and gum formation in storage; detergents are used for keeping carburetors clean and antirust are used to prevent corrosion in fuel system.

Advance Royalty. Payment made ahead of production in a mineral property that may or may not be recovered from future production.

Affiliate. An entity or associated company under the direct or indirect ownership, operation or control of another entity.

Affiliate Transactions. Transactions involving an affiliate company and its parent company where the parent company owns a controlling or substantial shares in the affiliate company.

Affiliated Marketer. A marketing company owned by an interstate pipeline or company with an interstate pipeline subsidiary that buys sells and resells gas.

Agent. A person entrusted with the business of another or acting by the authority of the principal on his behalf. An agent in this capacity does not have title to the property of the principal as his actions in this regard are subject to the control of the principal who takes responsibility for the transactions.

Aggregator. A company that specializes in consolidating a number of suppliers or markets into an aggregate group for purposes of pooling gas from various sources into packages for resale to end-users. Aggregator is also responsible for the planning, scheduling, billing, accounting, and settlement for gas or other petroleum products deliveries from the group of sellers and/or buyers.

Agreement. This refers to concord made by two or more parties that have entered into a contract where the terms and conditions relating to the transactions, which in this case, the sales and transportation of petroleum products, have been clearly defined or described.

Air Injection. This involves the injection of air into hydrocarbon formation to increase reservoir pressure. It is also known as enhanced recovery technique.

Alkylation. This is a refining process involving conversion of gaseous olefins and light into high-octane gasoline components. A chemical reaction involving the fixing of an alkyl radical onto a molecule.

All-Events Contract. Sales or transportation of gas volumes or services contract where the customer is required to take or pay even where the seller is unable to deliver, regardless of who is responsible for the failure.

Allocation. An approved consignment of crude oil or gas given to a company by regulatory authorities for resale or distribution to the domestic or international market. It is also the approved sharing of crude oil or petroleum products on a contractual or historic basis during scarcity. Allocation is sometimes adopted by a supplier to ensure equitable distribution of products to its customers. In times of scarcity, allocation is used as strategy to ensure availability of products in line with government's agency distribution plan.

Allowable. This is the approved production limit that member countries of the Organisation of Petroleum Exporting Countries (OPEC) are allowed. It is a strategy adopted to contain the price of crude oil. For example, when the price of crude oil is astronomically high, additional volumes are approved by members to curb the rise, and vice-versa.

Alternative Fuel. This is used mainly to describe "non-conventional" transportation fuels derived from natural gas, liquefied petroleum gas, compressed natural gas, methanol, etc.

Alternative-fuel vehicle (AFV). A vehicle designed to run on alternative fuel like compressed natural gas, methane blend and electricity. Such a vehicle could also be designed to run exclusively on "non-conventional" fuel or to operate on both non-conventional and conventional fuels.

American Petroleum Institute (API). API is an American trade association representing the oil and natural gas industry in that country. The Institute provides support for the oil and gas industry through its research and engineering work which form the basis for setting standards in the areas of operations and safety. It provides statistical information to relevant agencies and specifications for the manufacturing of oil field equipment.

Anniversary Date. One year from the date a lease agreement took effect, and by which time a renewal of rentals is due for payment to sustain the lease even in the absence of drilling or production.

Annual Contract Quantity. This is the quantity of gas a buyer undertakes to purchase from a seller during each contract year.

Anthropogenic. It is used within the context of global climatic change to refer to gaseous emissions induced by human activities and activities capable of altering climatic conditions.

API Gravity. This is the American Petroleum Institute classification of crude oil based on specific gravity, where the greater the gravity, the lighter the oil. It is the measurement of specific gravity of crude oil or condensate in degrees.

Appraisal Drilling. Drilling to determine physical extent, reserves and likely production rate of a reservoir, together with properties of oil or gas.

Appraisal Well. An oil well drilled during an appraisal drilling programme with a view to determining the reserves, production rate and physical extent of a field.

Aromatics. A class of hydrocarbons containing a minimum of one benzene ring as part of their structure. Most crude oils contain to some extent, aromatic hydrocarbon.

Arms-length Transactions. Sales or purchases' transactions involving two or more unaffiliated firms like the sales of gas by a producer to an unrelated company.

Artificial Lift. Any techniques, other than natural drives, for bringing oil to surface.

Asphalt. It is a cement-like material constituted mainly by bitumen and obtained through petroleum distillation process. Asphalt is black or dark-brown in colour and used for constructing roads.

Associated Gas. This refers to natural gas that is found together with crude oil in an oil field or in naturally occurring underground formations either as dissolved or solution gas within the oil-bearing strata or as gas cap gas above the oil zone. It is the higher, more volatile components obtained after the heavier and less volatile components have been extracted.

ASME. American Society of Mechanical Engineers (ASME). It is responsible for formulating codes and standards for the practice of mechanical engineering in various areas, including flanged fittings, pressure, temperature ratings, tolerances, dimensions, marking, testing and steel pipe flanges.

ASTM. American Society for Testing Materials responsible for developing standards for materials and test methods.

Atmospheric crude oil distillation. This involves separation of crude oil constituents at atmospheric pressure by heating to temperatures of about 600 degrees to 750 degrees Fahrenheit during refining process.

Authority for Expenditure (AFE). This refers to cost estimate for drilling and completing an oil well. It is usually prepared by a lease operator who then sends it to all the non-operators with working interest for approval before commencement of work.

Average Cost. This pertains to when the total cost of production is divided by the total quantity of oil or gas produced. What is left is the average cost.

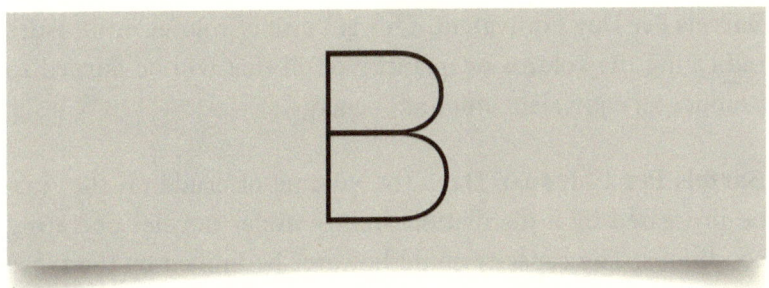

Balancing Item. This is the difference between the components of natural gas supply and the components of natural gas disposition or receipt due mainly to loss of quantities during transit or errors recorded during data reporting or computation.

Balancing Penalty. This is the scheduling and imbalance charges, penalties, fees or cashouts contained in a transporter's tariff, which may be assessed against a shipper for failure to satisfy the transporter's balance/ scheduling requirements.

Balance-sheet Financing. A conventional method for financing capital projects through debts based on the company's overall financial strength, using its assets as collateral or security.

Bar. This refers to the unit of measurement for specifying pressure of natural gas in pipelines. For example, one bar equals 0.987 standard atmospheric pressure.

Barrel. A crude oil measurement. This is a unit of volume equal to 120 litres or one drum or 42 U. S. gallons. The weight of a barrel is about 306 pounds or 5.80 million British thermal unit (Btu) of crude oil. In energy terms, one barrel of oil is about 6 million Btu.

Barrels Per Day Equivalent. This is a unit of volume or measure indicating the volume or quantity of oil that will be burned to produce an equivalent amount of energy.

Barrels Per Calendar Day. The volume of crude oil that can be processed by a distillation facility under normal operating conditions. The capacity could however be limited by the types and grades of inputs, products, environmental bottlenecks, maintenance and routine inspection which could lead to delay and interruption.

Barrels Per Stream Day. The maximum volume of crude oil that distillation facility can process within a 24-hour period when running at full capacity under optimal crude and product slate conditions without disruption of operations.

Base (Cushion) Gas. The required quantity of gas for a permanent inventory to support adequate reservoir pressures and deliverability rates during withdrawal season.

Base-load. The lowest load level of a utility (company) daily or annual gas supply to a customer on a year-round basis.

Basic Sediment and Water (BS&W). Impurities such as emulsified water, suspended particles from reservoir formation contained in oil coming out from a well.

Basin. A large natural depression on the earth's surface containing sediments which have been accumulated over a long interval haracterized by layers of rock usually from the sides to the centre.

Benzene. A colourless hydrocarbon liquid present in small proportion in some crude oil and made commercially from petroleum by the catalytic reforming of naphthenes in petroleum naphtha. It can be used to power motor vehicles, and its chemical symbol is C6H6.

Bid. An offer made by an applicant for an oil lease in accordance with prescribed guidelines and other conditions.

Bi-Fuel Vehicle. This is a vehicle designed or capable of operating on two separate fuel systems and these are mainly common with light-duty vehicles. Both fuels cannot be used at the same time, but one at a time. During scarcity of a particular fuel, drivers can switch to the other.

Bi-Gas. A process of creating or developing a means for making synthetic gas from coal. A synthetic gas is a substitute for natural gas for industrial and domestic energy needs.

Billing Period. This is the period preceding the time a meter was read and computed for the determination of the volume of fuel oil or gas consumed.

Biofuels. These are liquid fuels produced from plant feedstocks and used primarily for transportation.

Biogas. This is a combustible gas resulting from an anaerobic decomposition of organic material comprising primarily of hydrogen sulfide, carbon dioxide and methane.

Biomass Fuel. This is the conversion of a biomass into liquid or gaseous fuels like methane, methanol, ethanol or hydrogen.

Biomass Gas. This refers to a combustible gas made up of methane and carbon dioxide as a result of the action of micro- organisms on organic materials such as a landfill.

Bitumen. This is a mixture of mainly tar-like hydrocarbons that are heavier than pentane containing sulphur compounds. In its naturally occurring viscous state, it cannot be recovered at a commercial rate from a well.

Black Oil. Crude oil or heavy fuel ol from the bottom of the refining process as opposed to white oil.

Bleed. When liquid or gas is generally drained off through a bleeder, a valve.

Bleed Down/Off. This involves the release of pressure slowly from a well or from pressurized equipment.

Bloc. An area marked on a leasing map reflecting specific identity number, area, and latitude and longitude coordinates.

Blow-down. The making of gas and condensate simultaneously from outset of production.

Blow-out. This is the uncontrolled flow of gas, oil or other fluids from a well due to pressure beyond the ability of the wellhead valves to control.

Blow-out Preventer (BOP). High pressure heavy- duty valves (equipment) used in controlling pressures or shutting off an uncontrolled flow of hydrocarbons during drilling, completion, and work-over operations at wellhead to prevent accidental blow-outs.

Boiler. A tank containing water that is heated (either by natural gas or liquid fuels) or coal to produce steam or hot water for purposes of heating building space, producing electric power or industrial process heat.

Bonded Petroleum Imports. Petroleum import that is entered into customs bonded storage and which are not classified among import statistics. Such classification can only materialize if such product had been withdrawn from bonded storage with duty paid for domestic use or for use as fuel for ships and aircraft involved in international trade.

Bonus. An amount paid by a successful bidder to regulatory authorities of the oil and gas industry or to the owner of leasing rights for an oil lease.

Border Price. The price at which gas is sold at a country's border for purposes of export/import licensing and taxation.

Bottled Gas. This is liquefied petroleum gas (LPG) contained in a cylinder under a moderate pressure. It is a generic term used for butane, propane, or mixture of both under pressurised condition in a cylinder for domestic use.

Bottom-Hole Assembly. Components, together as a group, that make up lower end of drill-string (drill bit, drill collars, drill pipe and ancillary equipment).

Bradenhead. This refers to a casing-head used in confining gas in the well until it is released into a pipeline through an outlet.

Branded Product. This is petroleum product sold by a refiner to a purchaser with an authority to resell such a product under another brand name or trademark after reaching an agreement for such a deal.

Breeder. A nuclear reactor producing more fuel than the consumption required. It is used as a source of power.

British thermal unit (BTU). This is the measurement of the heating value of a fuel.

Broker. A person or company that acts as agent for a company which wants to buy or sell natural gas or one who buys and sells petroleum products or acquires leases on behalf of an oil and gas company.

Brown Field. A previously producing or mature oil field with declining output requiring upgrade for optimum productivity.

Buck Up. The tightening up two or more joints of drill pipes, like two threaded connections.

Budget Plan. An agreement between a domestic consumer and a fuel supplier for the payment of a fixed amount for fuel per month for a period of time.

Bulk Sale. Volume of gasoline transactions with individuals exceeding a truck load of product.

Bulk Tank. A large metal bin that usually holds a large amount of a certain mud additive on a drilling rig.

Bulk Station/Terminal. A facility used for the storage of petroleum products with a storage capacity of 50,000 barrels or more into which products are delivered by tankers, trucks, barge or pipeline.

Bunker Fuels. Petroleum products supplied to ships (fuel oil) and aircraft (kerosene-based jet fuel) both for domestic and international transactions.

Burner Tip. This is the point at which an industrial, commercial or residential customer takes gas from its gas supplier. It also means the point at which gas is ignited or the end of the gas delivery system.

Butane. Either of two saturated hydrocarbons, or alkanes, with chemical formula. In both compounds carbon atoms are joined in an open chain.

By-pass. Direct sales by gas producers, pipelines, or marketers to end-users.

By-product Coke Gas: A fuel-rich vapour that is a by- product of the coking process.

Bunker C Fuel Oil. Remnants or leftovers after other fuels have been extracted or distilled from crude oil. It is a heavy substance with high sulfur content and used mainly for power plants, large heating installations and ships.

Bundled (Re) Sales. Wholesale transaction of gas or sale to end-users at a single price which incorporates all transport and storage costs as well as the first-sale price of the gas commodity.

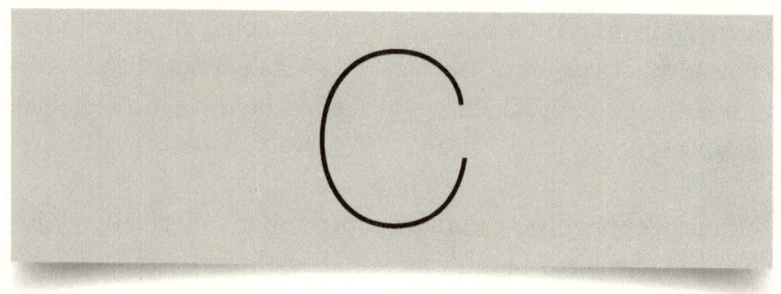

Calorific Value. This refers to the quantity of heat produced by the complete combustion of a fuel. This can be measured dry or saturated with water vapour.

Capital Cost. Cost of field development and plant construction together with the equipment required for industry operations.

Capping. A process of closing a well rightly to prevent hydrocarbons from escaping.

Carbon. The determinant of hydrocarbon's burning characteristics and qualities.

Carbon Dioxide. Colourless, odourless, and slightly acid- tasting gas, sometimes called carbonic acid gas, molecule of which consists of one atom of carbon joined to two atoms of oxygen.

Carbon Monoxide. Chemical compound of carbon and oxygen.

Carried Interest. An understanding involving two or more working entities with an entity (carried party) not sharing in lease revenue until a specific amount has been recovered by the other entity (carrying party) who pays costs applicable to the carried party's interest in the property but reimbursed later out of the revenue applicable to the carried party's interest.

Carrying Costs. These are costs associated with the retention of exploration and property rights after acquisition has occurred. It is usually before the occurrence of production. Some of such costs include legal cost for title defence, shut-in royalties, delay rentals, and ad valorem taxes on non- producing mineral properties.

Cash and Carry Transactions. These are transactions involving a consumer who provides his own container to purchase kerosene, fuel oil or bottled gas with a down payment through cash, cheque or credit card.

Casinghead. A fitting on a casing in a producing oil or gas well which regulates oil or gas flow rate as well as separate gas from oil.

Casinghead Gas (Oil Well Gas). Natural gas produced alongside crude oil from an oil well as against gas produced from a gas well. It is also called associated and dissolved gas or solution gas because it resides beneath the earth's surface together with crude oil.

Casing Perforation. Holes made in liner of a finished well to allow hydrocarbons to flow into production tube.

Casing Point. The point or time where a well has reached an acceptable depth where a decision as to whether to complete it for production or to plug and abandon it could be taken.

Catalytic Cracking. A refining process where high- boiling range fraction of petroleum (gas oil) is converted to gasoline, olefin feed for alkylation, distillate, fuel oil and fuel gas with the use of a catalyst and heat. It involves the breaking down of the larger, heavier, and more complex hydrocarbon molecules into simpler and lighter molecules. The gas oil is further used for recycling.

Catalytic Hydrocracking. A refining process for treating petroleum fractions from atmospheric or vacuum distillation units like naphthas, reformer feeds, residual fuel oil, heavy gas oil as well as other petroleum like gas oil, cat cracked naphtha, coker naphtha, etc. with catalysts and substantial quantities of hydrogen.

Catalytic Reforming. A refining process of using controlled heat and pressure with catalysts to rearrange certain hydrocarbon molecules, and in the process, convert paraffinic and naphthenic type hydrocarbons like low octane gasoline boiling range fractions, into petrochemical feedstocks and higher octane stocks suitable for blending into finished gasoline.

Cathodic Protection. Device used for protecting the integrity or minimizing rate of electrochemical corrosion of oil and gas pipelines, storage tanks, offshore installations and other related structures.

Cement. Pumped into space between casing and well bore wall in order to hold casing in place.

Choke. This is a heavy steel nipple used as a device for curtailing flow rate and maintaining control over an oil well during exploratory discovery testing. This is done by restricting the size of the opening through which the well produces.

Chlorofluorocarbon. Synthetic chemical that is odourless, non-toxic, non-inflammable, and chemically slow.

Christmas Tree. A decorated Christmas tree-like shape made up of pipes, fittings, gauges, controls and valves installed at the top of a gas or oil well at ground level for purposes of controlling and directing production flow rate of oil and gas from a well.

Circulation. Techniques for bringing cuttings from bottom of well bore to surface by continuously pumping drilling mud down through drill-string and up annulus during rotary drilling.

City Gate. A point or measuring station where gas passes from a main transmission pipeline system to a smaller gas pipeline distributing utility system for further distribution for local consumption.

Closed-In. A term referring to a well with the capacity to produce but currently not producing.

Coal Conversion. The changing or transformation of coal into synthetic gas or liquid fuels.

Coal Gas. A synthetically produced natural gas through the chemical reduction of coal at a coal gasification facility.

Coal Gasification. This is the conversion of coal into gas and the process involves the crushing of coal into powder which is further heated with steam and oxygen to produce gas. The gas is further refined to strip of sulfur content and other impurities to the barest minimum. The gas is used as fuel or processed further and concentrated into chemical or liquid fuel.

Coal Oil. The oil resulting from the distillation of bituminous coal.

Co-generation. This is the production of steam or heat through the sequential use of energy. It is a process where the heat generated from a production process is used as a source of energy for a subsequent conversion process. Natural gas could be used to fuel a cogeneration facility producing both steam and electricity.

Coiled Tubing. It is used for carrying out production tubing to bottom of well.

Coke. The remnants or leftovers of the product resulting from the incomplete burning of crude oil or coal. It is an important material for steel making.

Coking. It is a refining process where gasoline, distillates, and petroleum coke are produced from residual oils or the heavier products. The process involves the application of the coking unit or coker to heat up hydrocarbons to about 800 degrees Fahrenheit, causing the lighter products to vaporize and coke solidifies in a large drum, and further removed through a high-pressured jets of water. The coke can be used as industrial fuel and for power plant while the distillates can be further refined into heating oils and gasoline.

Coiled Tubing. Used to carry production equipment to bottom of well.

Commercial Well. An oil well or gas field considered capable of producing sufficiently, and lucrative enough to generate net income or profit from the operation (cost of drilling, equipping, completing, and operating expenses) within a reasonable time frame. An onshore production of 50 barrels a day could be said to be commercial given the cost elements ascribed to it. This could not be said of the same volume of production in an production where higher production cost will be incurred due to the expensive production facilities including pipelines that might be deployed.

Commingled Gas. Combination of gas from two or more sources into a single stream.

Commingling. This refers to the transportation of oil and gas from two or more different fields through a common pipeline. It also refers to when petroleum is produced from two or more reservoirs at different depths.

Compensator. It keeps drill-sting stationary while semi-submersible and derrick move.

Completion Fluid. The application of low-solids fluid or drilling mud when a well is at completion stage.

Completion (Well). A mechanically completed well ready for production. The process involved tubing, installation of valves, wellhead, etc. aimed at bringing a gas or oil well into production. Commencement of process is contingent upon reaching a level of depth where oil is believed to exist in the well.

Compliant Tower. It is a fixed rig structure used for offshore production of oil or gas. It comprises several rigid steel sections joined together by hinges to enable the tower sway under environmental loads. The rig consists of narrow, flexible (compliant) towers and a piled foundation supporting a conventional deck for drilling and production operations.

Compressed Natural Gas (CNG). Natural gas that is compressed under high pressure in a container but which also expands when it is released for use as fuel. It is increasingly being used as a vehicular fuel for cars, trucks and buses.

Compressor. It is used for increasing pressure of natural gas to facilitate easy flow through a transmission or distribution pipeline.

Compressor Station. Stations where gas is recompressed to ensure an even flow owing to the long distance it travels. Stations are usually located at about 60 to 80 kilometres along the transmission line.

Concession. This refers to the granting of acreage by a government to a company or an operator for exploration and development of petroleum fields under some specific conditions, among which are areas to be explored, duration, compensation, conditions for exploration, and sometimes, how landowners are to be compensated for the use of their land.

Condensate. Liquid mixture of pentane and higher hydrocarbons. It is light liquid hydrocarbons produced with natural gas but which are separated through a process of cooling, expansion, etc. When the natural gas is brought to the surface, the reduction in temperature and pressures causes the vapours to condense into a liquid. The liquids or condensate are extracted from raw natural gas through a process of condensation in a separation plant. These liquids include propane, butane, and heavier hydrocarbons for making gasoline, and are sold separately.

Conductor. Wide-diameter pipe from drilling platform to sea-bed to guide drilling and contain drilling fluid.

Continental Shelf. A sloping shallow point extending from the shore to the continental slope where the steepest descent of the ocean bottom begins. It is an area where water is less than 200 metres or 600 feet deep.

Contingent Resources. Contingent resources are unclassified oil reserves not commercially recoverable but which have the potential to be recoverable from known accumulations within a particular timeframe, using established technology. There is usually a sustained effort to eliminate these contingencies aimed at moving the contingent resources to reserves.

Conventional Fueled Vehicle. A vehicle that runs on petroleum-based products like premium motor spirit or petrol or diesel.

Conventional Gas. This is natural gas as occurred in nature and which can be produced under current technologies at a cost within its current market value. It is different from synthetic gas which does not naturally occur.

Conversion. This is a refining process involving the breaking up of large molecules into smaller parts to produce lighter compounds. It also means a device by which a conventional fuel vehicle is changed to alternative fuel vehicle.

Converted Vehicle. A vehicle originally designed to run on gasoline but later modified or altered to use an alternative fuel.

Coring. When special tools are deployed to extract samples of rock from a well.

Correlative Rights. Rights on multiple ownership of oil and or gas within a common reservoir.

Cost, Insurance and Freight (CIF). Price attaches to the product delivered at the importing terminal.

Cracking. This is a refinery process involving the breaking down of large, heavy, complex hydrocarbon molecules in heavy oils into simpler and lighter molecules for purposes of producing variety of fuels. The process is a major means for upgrading heavy oils into various fuels.

Critical Pressure. This is the required minimum pressure for liquefying a gas at its critical temperature.

Critical Temperature. This refers to the temperature level beyond which a gas cannot be liquefied irrespective of the pressure.

Crossover sub. When different sizes and types of drill pipe or other components allowed by sub to be joined.

Crude Oil. This is unprocessed or unrefined liquid petroleum in natural underground reservoirs consisting of natural mixture of hydrocarbons, black in colour with variable specific gravity and viscosity. It could be produced through refining process into wide range of petroleum products, namely, gasoline or petrol, diesel, dual purpose kerosene or jet fuels, heating oils, lubricants, propane, butane, ethane, asphalt, etc. There are different types of crude oils and each is characterized by the value and the different mixture of hydrocarbon molecules. The value is determined by its quality and quantity as it ranges from very light (high in potential gasoline) to very heavy (high in potential residual oil). Sulfur is an important characteristic in crude oil. Crude oil that is characterized by high sulfur content is low in value.

Crude Oil F. O. B. Price. This refers to the actual price charge of crude oil at country of origin's port of loading, including deductions (discounts or rebates) or additions of premiums as appropriate.

Crude Oil Input. The total crude oil volume discharged into the processing units of refineries.

Crude Oil Landed Cost. This refers to the price of crude oil at the port of discharge, including charges relating to purchases, transportation, and insurance on the cargo from the point of purchase to the port of discharge. This however excludes charges like import tariffs, demurrage, etc. incurred at the port of discharge.

Crude Oil Losses. These are crude oil losses resulting from spills, fires, contamination, leakages, pipeline vandalisation, etc.

Crude Oil Stocks. These are crude oil stocks held at refineries, in pipelines and pipeline terminals but exclude those on leases for storage facilities near the wells.

Cryogenics. Method or technique which utilizes extremely low temperatures to produce natural gas liquids, from a raw gas stream.

Cubic Foot of Gas or Standard Cubic Foot of Gas. This pertains to a unit of volume or measurement of natural gas.

Curtailment Policy. A policy of rationalization where there is a deliberate reduction in volume of gas or service to specified customers due to inadequate supply or inability to meet demand.

Daily Drilling Report. Daily record of operations in a drilling rig which is transmitted to the head-office through email, fax, telephone or radio.

Day Trade. This refers to sale and purchase of futures contract on the same day. It also refers to the sale and purchase of natural gas on a daily basis.

Danger. Risk of injury.

Dangerous Occurrence. Readily identifiable event with potential to cause an accident or disease to persons at work and public or of significant actual of potential material damage.

Dealer Mark-Up. The difference between the price a dealer of petrol or gasoline pays his supplier and the price he sells to consumers. He defrays overhead costs including wages and rent from this mark-up.

Deep-Water Discovery. An offshore discovery located in at least 200 metres of water.

Dedicated (Contracted) Owner. The owner of an oil and gas well who is also a party to a contract for the sale of gas produced from that well.

Dedicated Reserves. This refers to the volume of recoverable gas reserves possessed by an utility or pipeline company. Reserves here include gas contained in underground storage and those based on contractual commitment with independent producers for sale of gas from a given well or field to a particular buyer.

Dedicated Vehicle. This is a vehicle configured to operate only on alternative fuel like compressed natural gas.

Deepest Total Depth. This refers to the distance from a surface reference point of an oil well to the deepest point of penetration. This is ascertained through the measurement of the well. It is also referred to as depth of deepest production.

Deep Gas. Natural gas found 15,000 feet and beyond beneath the earth's surface.

Deep-Water Discovery. This refers to an offshore discovery located beyond the continental shelf.

Deep-Water Ports. These are ports with shore facilities capable of accommodating Very Large Crude Carriers (VLCCs) and Ultra Large Crude Carriers (ULCCs) for loading and discharging of cargoes.

Deferred Fuel Cost. An incurred expenditure not recognized as a cost for a given period but deferred to future period before being written off. This is done for purposes of book-keeping.

DeficiencyPayment. Payment made by agas purchaser in fulfillment of a "take or pay" clause contained in a Gas Sales and Purchase Agreement (GSPA). Deficiency payments are induced by the inability of buyers to take a specified minimum volume of gas in accordance with the GSPA, hence are obliged to pay for the deficient volume of gas.

Degasser. The equipment used to eliminate undesirable and surplus gas from a drilling fluid or liquid.

Degasification System. The process of removing methane from a coal seam which could not be terminated by standard ventilation fans and which usually exposes coal miners to hazard. These methods may be used prior to or during mining activities.

Dehydrator, Natural Gas. It is equipment designed to remove entrained water from gas, as it is imperative for gas to be relatively free of water to meet pipeline specifications.

DelayedCoking. The process of thermally decomposing heavier crude oil fractions in increased temperatures and pressure to produce a mixture of lighter oils and petroleum coke. The light oils can further be processed in refineries while the coke can be used as fuel or in the manufacturing of aluminium or steel.

Delay Rentals. This is the payment made to a lessor as privilege for continuing with a lease without drilling on it. Such payment is made annually where drilling does not take place.

Delineation Well. A well that is drilled from a distance with a view to determining the physical state, reserves and production rate of a new oil or gas field.

Deliverability. The amount of gas that a pipeline company or producer supplies within its delivery capacity to meet its obligations for a given period from currently committed sources of supply. The availability of gas from these sources of supply is usually governed by the physical capabilities of these sources to deliver gas by the terms of existing gas-purchase-contracts.

Delivered Cost. This refers to the cost of fuel inclusive of related expenses, namely, transportation charges, taxes, invoice price of fuel, commissions, insurance, and expenses associated with leased or owned equipment used for transporting fuel.

Delivered Gas. The transfer of gas (natural, liquefied, synthetic or supplemental) from the facilities of a utility company to another or to an end-user.

Delivery Point. The point at which sellers deliver gas to buyers.

Demand Charge. This is the amount paid by a customer to enjoy rights to be supplied certain maximum volume of gas at any time during the year without interruption. Customers who purchase gas on an "interruption" basis do not pay a demand charge.

Demand (Utility). This refers to the level at which natural gas is delivered to end-users at a specified point in time.

Demonstrated Reserves. This refers to proven and "indicated" reserves which can be estimated with reasonable certainty based on current economic conditions. These reserves which are found in productive reservoirs in existing field react positively to improved recovery techniques.

Demurrage. This is the charge paid to a vessel owner or operator for delay of a vessel at the sea port beyond the specified time of stay for discharging or loading.

Depletion. This refers to the shrinkage or decline in the value of an oil or gas well resulting from production operations.

Depletion Storage Field. This refers to an exhausted gas or oil field used for storing natural gas. It is a sub- surface natural geological reservoir.

Deregulation. This is the termination or removal of controls or conditions regulating the operations of a business. The process involves amendment of regulatory policies and laws and it is mainly designed to promote competition in the market.

Derrick. A vertically erected metal tower above a well- aimed at lifting and lowering tubes and tools into the well.

Derrickman. He provides support to the driller at the top of the derrick. Typically, his job entails guiding the stands of drill pipe into the fingers at the top of the derrick while removing the drill string from the hole, or more.

Desalting. This is the process of removing salt from crude oil. It is usually done before the commencement of refining and commercialization of the crude.

Desulfurization. This pertains to the removal of sulfur from products like oil, flue gases or molten metals. It is a refining process aimed at raising the quality of petroleum products by the removal of sulfur content from crude oils. Some sulfur compounds are corrosive hence are factors in air pollution, engines, furnaces and boilers.

Detergent Oils. These are lubricating oils with special detergent-dispersing properties used for cleaning engines and industrial equipment.

Development. A process of turning an oil or gas proven field into a full-fledged producing field. It involves the construction of access roads, installation of separating and gathering facilities as well as drilling.

Development Drilling. This is the process of determining the specific size, grade and configuration of oil deposit prior to the determination of whether it can be commercially developed. This excludes solution mining drilling, secondary development drilling and production-related underground and open pit drilling.

Development Well. An oil well drilled to a known producing formation in a previously discovered field or gas reservoir for purposes of completing the intended spacing pattern of production.

Deviated Well. This refers to a horizontal well that is drilled at an angle to vertical (over 80 degrees).

Diesel-Electric Plant. This is a generating station which uses diesel engines to drive its electric generators.

Diesel Engine. This is a non-spark-ignition engine in which fuel is ignited through its injection into a heated air. It is generally referred to as a compression-ignition piston engine.

Diesel Fuel. This refers to fuel made up of distillates derived from petroleum refining process or during blends of such distillates along with residual oil used in motor vehicles. The boiling point and specific gravity of diesel fuels are higher than petrol.

Diesel Oil. This is an extract from petroleum product. It is constituted mainly by aliphatic hydrocarbons. It is similar to gas in terms of volatility.

Direct Purchase. Purchase of gas by end-users directly from producers rather than from distributors.

Direct Sale. Sale of natural gas by producers on a contractual basis to end users, rather than to distributors for resale. Such sales contracts are usually for a particular time frame.

Directional Drilling. This involves the deflection of a drill bit in order to drill at an angle from a vertical.

Directional (deviated) Well. A well specifically shifted from a vertical, using controlled angles to get to an objective spot as against below the surface location. A directional well may be an initial original hole which deviates from the original bore a some point below the surface.

Discharged Fuel. Irradiant fuel discharged or separated from a nuclear reactor during refueling.

Discovery. This refers to a find of substantial quantities of oil or gas.

Discovery Date. The date scheduled for the discovery of a new oil field.

Discovery Well. This refers to the first oil or gas well undergoing exploration in a new field (exploratory well) where hydrocarbons are found. In other words, an exploratory well that finds hydrocarbons.

Discretionary Gas. This refers to gas produced or shut-in at the discretion of the operator. This excludes casinghead gas.

Disposition, natural gas. This is the disposal of natural gas as well as synthetic and supplemental gas or any other gaseous components from a company's facilities for specific purposes including distribution of the gas to end-users.

Disposition, petroleum. The transfer or removal of petroleum products from supply stream by way of exports, distribution for domestic consumption, stock change or crude oil losses.

Disposal Well. A well used for the disposal of saltwater into an underground formation.

Dissolved Gas. Natural gas that is found mixed with oil in naturally occurring formations underground and which can be developed for commercial use. It is also referred to as Solution Gas.

Distillate Oil. This refers to a crude oil that has been distilled, and which as a result, transformed into a light petroleum product. It is used for heating in homes.

Distillation. This is the first stage of a refining process involving the heating of crude oil which is subsequently cooled and condensed into liquid fractions of petrol (gasoline), kerosene, diesel, etc.

Distillation unit (atmospheric). The section of a refinery plant that processes crude oil or mixture of other hydrocarbons at approximately atmospheric conditions. The distillation unit is constituted mainly by a pipe still for vaporizing the crude oil and a fractionation tower for separating the vaporized hydrocarbon components in the crude oil into fractions with different boiling ranges.

Distribution. The delivery of gas or refined products through pipeline or trucks from transmission network to retail customers.

Distributor. A company engaged in the sale, supply and delivery of natural gas to end-users through trucks or pipeline system. A distributor is also known as a jobber, wholesaler or reseller who owns the petroleum products he sells to retailers and sometimes, leases his storage and distribution facilities to retailers with service stations.

Division Order. A document mandating a purchaser to pay the owners of oil and gas for a specified volume in a particular well. A Division Order document usually contains the name of the product or property, operator, effective date, legal description, decimal interest and type of interest.

Downstream. This refers to the areas of the oil and gas industry relating to refining, marketing, distribution, shipping and trucking of petroleum products as distinct from exploration and production in the Upstream.

Drilling. This is the boring of a hole to determine availability of possible commercially recoverable hydrocarbons. Drilling involves the deployment of rig and crew for drilling, completion, suspension, capping, production testing, deepening, sidetracking, redrilling, reconditioning, plugging and abandoning of a well. It also entails the conversion of a well to a source, observation and injection as well as geological studies of strata and their succession and other related environmental studies.

Drilling Arrangement. This involves a contractual agreement under which the owner of a property with working interest (assignor) assigns part of the working interest in the property to another party (assignee) who in turn, based on a proviso, agrees to develop the property.

Drilling Crew. This comprises a driller, a derrickhand, and two or more helpers who provide support to a drilling or workover rig each day.

Drill Cuttings. During a drilling process, the small pieces of rock created as the drill bit moves through underground formations is known as drill cuttings.

Drilling Mud. Mixture of base substance and additives used to lubricate drill bit and to counter act natural pressure in formation. Drilling mud provides circulation, flushing rock cuttings from bottom of well bore to surface.

Drill In. This involves penetration of the productive formation after the casing is set and cemented on top of the pay zone.

Drilling Platform. A structure designed to provide support for drilling equipment, supplies, and operations during offshore wells drilling.

Drilling Rig. This refers to a drilling unit or derrick that is not permanently fixed to the seabed. It usually contains a giant winch for lifting and lowering the drill pipe, a round table rotating the drill pipe and bit, and an engine that drives the winch and rotary table.

Drilling Riser. It is a long metal or plastic pipe that transports oil from the sea floor to the production facility above. In other words, it is a conduit that provides a temporary extension of a subsea oil well to a surface drilling facility. Drilling risers are categorised into two types: marine drilling risers used with subsea blowout preventer (BOP) and generally used by floating drilling vessels; and tie-back drilling risers used with a surface BOP and generally deployed from fixed platforms or very stable floating platforms like a spar or tension leg platform.

Drill Stem Test. It is a process of ascertaining a formation's content (gas, oil or water) and production potential before casing is installed in the well.

Drum Cycle. This refers to the length of time involved during petroleum coking process in heating the coke drum to the extent of safely introducing hot hydrocarbons, transforming the raw material into solid petroleum coke, and removing the solid coke from the drum. The process is repeated all over again thereafter.

Dry Gas. Remnants of natural gas volume free of liquid hydrocarbons after the removal of all liquids including water vapour. It is predominantly methane with minor amounts of ethane, propane and butane with little or no heavier hydrocarbons. It is also known as lean gas.

Dry Gas Field. A gas field or reservoir with dry or lean gas content and also containing small volume of condensate.

Dry Hole. Unsuccessful well, drilled without finding commercial quantities of hydrocarbons. An exploratory or development well that does not contain gas or oil and which also lacks favourable conditions that can support commercial quantities of exploitable hydrocarbons, making it financially unworthwhile to produce. Dry holes are also referred to as "dusters."

Dry Hole Charge. This refers to an amount charged as expense of a previously capitalized cost after the conclusion of an unsuccessful drilling exercise.

Dry Hole Contribution. Payment in form of cash or acreage made for well test and evaluation data based on agreement in connection with an unsuccessful test well.

Dry Natural Gas. Remnants or leftovers after liquefiable hydrocarbon portion has been removed from a gas stream.

Drill-String. Series of connected 9 metre length drill pipes (joints).

Dual Completion. The completion of a well designed to produce from two separate reservoirs.

Dual Fuel (Bi-Fuel) Vehicle. A vehicle that can operate on two different fuels like compressed natural gas, diesel or petrol (gasoline).

Due Diligence. Prudent examination and analysis of oil and gas properties before acquisition.

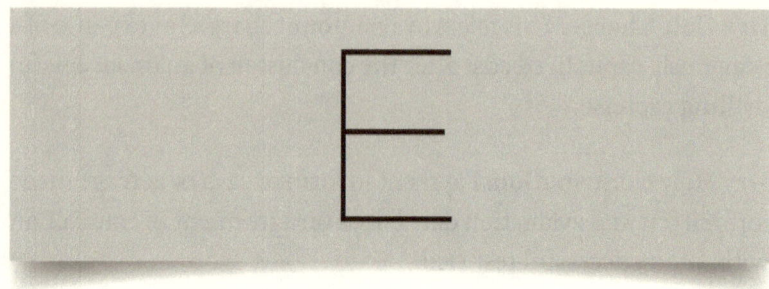

Easement. A temporary right granted to a non-owner of a land for purpose of laying a pipeline from a well or for other purpose.

Economic Efficiency. This is a term used for actions that raise the overall net value of production and consumption of goods and services. Economic efficiency manifests when prices of products and services reflect their marginal costs. The gains of economic efficiency are achieved through cost reductions, among other factors.

Economically Recoverable Resource Estimate. An evaluation of hydrocarbon potentials of an oil and gas field, taking into consideration, the physical and technological constraints on production as well as impact of exploration, development costs and market price on investment.

Effluent. The blending of water, oil, gas and sand discharged from a well.

Elasticity of Demand. This is the ratio of percentage change in the volume of product demanded to the percentage change in price.

Emissions. A pollutant waste or substance discharged or released to the atmosphere or water as a result of a process or action.

Ending Stocks. Crude oil and petroleum products primary stocks held in storage as at 12 midnight on the last day of the month. Such stocks are usually held in storage at tank farms, bulk terminals, refineries, natural gas, leases, pipelines and gas processing plants.

End User. Individuals or utilities which purchase petroleum products for own consumption other than for re-sale.

Energy/Fuel Diversity Policy. A policy that supports the development of energy technologies aimed at diversifying energy supply sources in order to reduce dependence on petroleum fuels.

Energy/Fuel Security Policy. A policy that recognizes the risk associated with reliance on sources of fuel located in remote and unstable regions of the world together with the benefits of domestic and diverse fuel sources.

Energy Source. Any substance like petroleum, natural gas, electricity, biomass, wind, etc., that can be processed to supply heat or power.

Energy Supplier. Energy companies supplying natural gas, fuel oil, kerosene, LPG for household or domestic use.

Enhanced Reach. Deviated wells (over 65 degrees) from vertical and reach out horizontally more than twice vertical depth.

Enhanced Oil Recovery. A recovery technique involving the use of any process to increase the amount of oil removed from a reservoir (such as water flooding or gas injection into existing wells) other than by the natural pressure in a reservoir.

Environment. This refers to our surroundings or locality and the natural and living constituents therein, namely, earth, air, weather, plants, and animals.

Environmental Impact Assessment. A systematic assessment of the likely impact of a project on the surrounding environment prior to or during operations or construction. Such assessment is also expected to make provision for necessary mitigating measures to enhance the environmental and social conditions.

Environmental Impact Statement. A sequential documentation of information required for the evaluation of the impact of a project on the environment. It informs and guides stakeholders including regulatory authorities and the public of the ways to avoid or minimize likely adverse impacts resulting from the project as well as ways of improving the quality of the environment.

Environmental Remediation. This is the process of restoring the environment back to its original form prior to commencement of operations or construction work. This includes restoration of contaminated soil, plants, rehabilitation of waste site, treatment of ground and surface water, etc.

E & P. Exploration and Production. This is the upstream aspect of the oil and gas industry.

Equity Crude Oil. The proportion of production a concession owner possess the contractual and legal right to retain.

Esters. Compounds formed by combination of acids and alcohols.

Ethane. A colourless and odourless gaseous hydrocarbon. It is extracted from natural gas and refinery gas streams.

Ethanol. This is a colourless and flammable oxygenated hydrocarbon produced from ethylene or from fermentation of various sugars derived from carbohydrates in agricultural products.

Ethylene. An olefinic hydrocarbon used as a petrochemical feedstock for consumer goods and various chemical applications. It is derived from petrochemical or refinery processes.

Excess Gas. Surplus amount of gas in a specified volume that a purchaser takes monthly.

Exchange Agreement. This refers to an agreement between two companies for the delivery of crude oil, natural gas or other petroleum products by one company to the other in exchange for an equivalent volume or heat content from the second party.

Expected Ultimate Reserves. Estimate of a cumulative volume of oil and gas reserves recoverable during the life of a well or field in a reservoir.

Expense Bearing Interest. Property interest in the oil and gas industry that is subject to production expense.

Expense Free Interest. Property interest in the oil and gas industry that is not subject to production expense.

Exploration. The process of finding oil prior to development. It involves geological and geophysical surveys; drilling for purpose of locating an oil or gas reservoir; and drilling of additional wells to delineate a reservoir after discovery. These measures determine the viability of commencing with development and production.

Exploration Drilling. Drilling exercise carried out to ascertain possible presence of hydrocarbons in a particular structure.

Exploration Phase. The phase of operation pertaining to oil search carrying out detailed geophysical and geological surveys. This phase precedes exploration drilling.

Exploration Well. A wildcat well drilled to find and produce oil or gas in an unproven area.

Extensions. Reserves credited to previously productive reservoir with enhanced volume resulting from additional new well drilling.

Extraction Loss. Reduction in volume and energy content of natural gas due to the removal of natural gas liquid constituents like ethane, butane and propane.

Extractive Industries. Industries whose activities involve prospecting and exploring of natural resources and this may also include the acquisition, development and production of the resources. Such industries do not include agriculture and others involved in resources of a regenerative nature.

Farm In. The acquisition of an oil bloc or field along with all or part of the financial commitment for the drilling of an exploration well. The transfer of part of an oil or gas interest in consideration for an agreement by transferee to meet certain expenditure that would otherwise have to be undertaken by licensee.

Farm Out. An arrangement used primarily in the oil and gas industry in which the owner or lessee assigns or partially assigns an oil bloc or field to an operator for drilling purposes.

Farm Out Agreement. A deal between owner (farmer) of an oil field and an operator (farmee) in which the farmer accepts to assign all or part to the farmee to drill well(s).

Farm Out Area. This refers to the area covered by a specified oil bloc or field.

Farm Out Facilities. The property and equipment within a specified oil bloc or field, which a farmor hands over to a Farmee.

Fatal Accident Frequency Rate (FAFR). The number of fatalities per 100 million man hours worked.

Fatality. Death resulting from work related injury or illness. **Fatality Rate.** Number of fatalities per 1000 employees. **Feeder Line.** A gathering line or pipeline that is tied into a trunk line.

Feedstock. Raw material or natural gas liquids supplied to or processed in a refining or chemical plant.

Field. A specified geographic area or underground productive formation containing single or multiple reservoirs. In other words, a geographical area under which an oil or gas reservoir lies.

Field Appraisal. The determination of the quantity of reserve levels and production capacity of a newly discovered reservoir.

Field Discovery Year. The year in which the economic viability of a field was first acknowledged as containing recoverable accumulation of oil and gas.

Field Production. Production of crude oil on leases or production of natural gas liquids at natural gas processing plants. It also represents the blending of fuel ethanol into finished petrol or premium motor spirit; and the supply of other hydrocarbons and their blending components.

Field Separation Facility. A surface installation designed to recover lease condensate from a produced natural gas stream usually originating from more than one lease and managed by the operator of one or more of these leases.

Field Rules. Rules pertaining to spacing and production for the common reservoir for the whole area.

Flash Point. Lowest temperature at which vapour above a flammable liquid can be ignited.

Flush Production. This is the extraction of oil from a well using only the natural pressure within the reservoir.

Fire Flooding. A method of recovering heavy, viscous oil. A portion of the underground oil is burned in place by pumping huge quantities of air into the formation.

Firm Delivery. This refers to the sales of gas under an agreed term where the seller is under obligation to deliver gas. The buyer under this circumstance, is also under obligation to accept delivery within the agreed specifications as per quality and quantity.

Firm Service. Service offered with a guarantee of uninterrupted gas supply.

Firm Storage Service. Pipeline storage service that is not subject to a prior claim by another customer or class or service.

Fishing. The process of retrieving objects like broken drill string or tools from a borehole.

Fixed Platforms. These are stand built on large steel or concrete legs that are fitted directly onto the seabed for the production oil or gas. It is made up of a welded tubular steel jacket, deck, and surface facility with the jacket and deck making up the foundation for the surface.

Flange. A piping system formed from the joining of pipes, valves, pumps and other equipment. Flanges which are usually welded or screwed provide easy access for cleaning, inspection or modification. Flanged joints are made by bolting together two flanges with a gasket between them to provide a seal.

Flare Bleeder. An instrument or device used for evacuating and burning of unused gases.

Flare Gas. Burning of unwanted gas from an oil field, production sites or at gas processing plants for technical reasons.

Flaring. The burning of hydrocarbon gases for commercial or technical reasons.

Flare Stack. Steel structure at a processing facility from which gas is flared.

Flexible-Fuel Vehicle. A vehicle designed with a single fuel tank to run on different blends of unleaded gasoline with either ethanol or methanol.

Flooding. A recovery method for increasing production in an existing oil field through the injection of water into the oil wells around the field's perimeter in order to create a pressure front to flush the oil to the centre of the field.

Flow Assurance System. It is designed to ensure uninterrupted flow of hydrocarbon between facilities connected by pipelines.

Flowline. This is an "intra-field" pipeline used in connecting subsea wellheads and manifolds to production facilities within a particular field. Generally, it is the surface pipe through which oil or gas travels from a well to processing equipment or storage.

Flue Gas. This is a fuel that is derived from the combustion of a fuel that is emitted to the flue.

Flue Gas Desulfurization. Equipment, usually scrubbers, used for removing sulfur oxides from the combustion gases of a boiler plant before discharge into the atmosphere.

Fluid Catalytic Cracking. This is the refining process of breaking down the larger, heavier, and more complex hydrocarbon molecules into simpler and lighter molecules for purposes of increasing the volume of petrol or gasoline from crude oil, among others.

Fluid Injection. The process of pumping fluid into a producing formation in order to increase or maintain reservoir pressure, and by extension, production.

Force Majeure. A contractual provision in a delivery agreement stating the conditions under which a party's obligations are waived if compliance are hindered by conditions deemed to be beyond the control of the supplier, namely, crisis, flood, war, fire or other natural disasters.

Foreign Access. This relates to proved reserves of crude, condensate, and natural gas liquids that are set aside for a long-term supply agreements with foreign governments or authorities with the company or one of its affiliates or subsidiaries acting as producer.

Formation. A layer of rock with varying degree of thickness with distinct texture or mineral composition.

Formation. A group of intermingled beds or separate layer of rock.

Formation Damage. The reduction in permeability in reservoir rock caused by the infiltration of drilling or treating fluids into the area adjacent to the wellbore.

Formation Fluid. Fluid like oil, gas, or water that exists in a subsurface formation.

Formation Pressure. Formation pressure occurs at the bottom of a well when it is shut in at the wellhead.

Formation Water. This refers to salt water underlying gas and oil in a formation.

Fossil Fuel. This is fuel formed in the ground from the remains of living cell organisms or dead plants and animals during pre-historic times. Some of these fuels which formations take millions of years under high temperature and pressure include oil, natural gas, coal or their by-products.

Fossil Fuel Plant. A plant which uses fuels like petroleum, natural gas or coal as its source of energy.

FPSO. It means floating production storage and offloading (unit). It is a floating vessel used for production and processing of oil and gas offshore by the oil and gas industry. It is also used for the storage of oil.

Frac Oil. Oil injected into a well during fracturing exercise which could be recovered through subsequent production.

Fractional Distillation. This is a basic refinery process involving the processing or refining of crude oil into petroleum products which are further separated out based on their boiling points.

Fracturing. The process of increasing production rates from a reservoir through the breaking down of a formation by pumping fluid (crude oil, diesel, water, or chemical) at very high pressures.

Fractionation. The process of removing liquid hydrocarbons from gas stream as well as separating specific liquid hydrocarbons from each other.

Free-On-Board (FOB). An FOB price in the international LNG market applies to the delivered product at the terminal of the exporting nation.

Fresh Feed Input. Energy sources such as crude oil, natural gas, and other hydrocarbons that are put into processing units at a refinery processed into a particular unit for the first time. For example, by-product of crude oil distillation unit put into a catalytic cracking unit for the first time.

Fresh Feeds. Crude oil distillation or other petroleum products fed to a processing unit for the first time.

Fuel. Any substance or material used to produce heat or energy, including petroleum, coal, and natural gas as well as other consumable materials like uranium, biomass and hydrogen.

Fuel Cell. A device capable of converting natural gas or other gaseous fuels directly into electricity and heat through an electrochemical process which avoids the energy losses associated with combustion and the spinning or reciprocation of mechanical parts.

Fuel Cycle. Stages of fuel utilization in sequential order involving extraction, transformation, transportation, and combustion.

Fuel Efficiency. The ratio of energy generated by a fuel for a particular work to the available energy in the fuel.

Fuel Gas. This is a synthetic gas with less energy content compared to quality gas obtained from pipeline. It is used for heating or cooling.

Fuel Injection. A fuel delivery system which allows petrol or gasoline to be pumped to one or more valves or fuel injectors under high pressure.

Fuel Oil. This is a form of petroleum product burned to generate heat or power in an engine, furnace or firebox after being heavily distilled in the refining process.

Fuel Purchase Agreement. An agreement made between a company and a fuel dealer which stipulates that the company agrees to purchase its fuel from the fuel provider with clearly spelt out terms and conditions.

Fuel and Shrinkage. This is the difference between the volume of gas produced at the wellhead and the gas that flows into a pipeline that could provide energy to on lease equipment or removal of solution gas.

Full Well Stream. Production from a well prior to any separation of the stream's components.

Futures. An obligation or contract entered into to buy or sell a specific quantity of oil or gas at a particular price in a specific month.

Gallon. It is a unit of volume used for measuring fuel oil. One barrel equals 42 gallons.

Gas. This refers to gaseous fuel like natural gas, coke-oven gas, blast-furnace gas, and refinery gas.

Gas Cap. The upper portion of reservoir rock of a gas field. The gas extracted during oil production could be injected into the gas cap to enhance hydrocarbon recovery.

Gas Contract. An agreement for the sale or purchase of gas.

Gas Cooled Fast Breeder Reactor: A fast breeder reactor that is cooled by a gas under pressure.

Gas Cycling. A recovery process which increases the production of condensate and natural gas liquids from a gas field.

Gas Detector. Instrument for detecting the presence of gas.

Gas Drive. This is a secondary recovery method which injects natural gas into an oil reservoir to move oil towards the producing well.

Gas Field. A field containing natural gas without the presence of oil.

Gas Gathering Line. A pipeline which transports gas from production point to a transmission line or mainline.

Gas Gathering System. A system of pipelines used for collecting gas from numerous wells from where it is piped to a major processing system or transmission pipelines.

Gas Grid. A network of gas transmission and distribution pipelines through which gas is transported to end users.

Gas Injection. The process of pumping back separated associated gas into a reservoir to maintain the reservoir pressure, a process which leads to increased flow of oil from wells.

Gas Lift. The process of lifting fluid from a well by injecting gas down the well through tubing.

Gas Lost. Natural gas that is avoidably wasted owing to flaring and which could otherwise have been retained in the production system for sale or put to other uses.

Gas Measurement. Calculation of volumes of natural gas by the use of conversion factors of standard pressure and temperature. The standard pressure is 14.73 pounds per square inch while the standard temperature is 60 degrees Fahrenheit.

Gasohol. A mixture of finished motor gasoline containing between 5 to 10 percent alcohol (generally ethanol or methanol).

Gas Oil. An oil distilled from the refining process and which is often used as diesel fuel.

Gas-Oil Ratio (GOR). The volume of gas at atmospheric pressure produced per barrel of oil.

Gasoline. The light petroleum product obtained from the refining of crude oil. It is a volatile, flammable and liquid hydrocarbon mixture used as fuel in internal combustion engines or motor vehicles.

Gas Processing. The separation of gas from oil together with the removal of liquid hydrocarbons such as propane and butane, toxic or corrosive substances such as hydrogen sulfide and carbon dioxides.

Gas Processing Plant. A facility designed to extract liquefiable hydrocarbons from natural gas or in which natural gas liquids are separated from natural gas with additional function of controlling the quality of the processed natural gas stream.

Gasifier. A device for converting solid fuel into gaseous fuel.

Gas Reserves. The original proven recoverable gas available in a formation, and which has been proven by production.

Gasification. A method for converting solid fuel like coal, wastes, biomass, petroleum into a gas that can be burned to generate power or processed into chemicals and fuels. It is also known as pyrolitic distillation or pyrolysis.

Gas-to-Liquids (GTL). A process which combines the carbon and hydrogen elements in natural gas molecules to form synthetic liquid petroleum products like diesel. It also refers to the conversion of natural gas to liquid form for ease of transportation, and it is usually re- converted back to natural gas before utilization.

Gas Treatment. The removal of impurities, condensate, hydrogen sulphide and natural gas liquids from natural gas.

Gas Turbine. A rotary motor in which combusted, pressurized gas is directed against a series of blades connected to a shaft, which forces the shaft to turn to generate mechanical energy.

Gas Utility. This refers to any person dealing with or authorized to deal with the distribution of natural gas through pipelines, trucks or ships.

Gas Well. A well which contains only gas and which is produced without associating or blending with crude oil. It also refers to a well which produces hydrocarbon liquids with major part formed by condensation from gas with the remaining being crude oil. Besides, any well which produces more than 100,000 cubic feet of natural gas for each barrel of crude oil from the same producing formation, is regarded as a gas well.

Gate Station. A point where the pressure of natural gas being transported from a transmission system to a distribution system is lowered to enable further conveyance of the product through small diameter and low pressure pipelines.

Gatherer. A company primarily engaged in the collection of natural gas from well or field lines for delivery to a natural gas processing plant for a fee. Such companies also provide compression, dehydration and treating services.

Gathering. The process of collecting gas from several wells before delivery to a transmission pipeline.

Geologic Assurance. State of certainty as to the availability of quantity of resources based on the quality of geologic data.

Geologic Consideration. Conditions in coal deposit or in the rocks and these are evaluated based on current state of technology and regulations.

Geological and Geophysical Costs. These are costs incurred in the course of geological and geophysical studies, and these include equipment, rights of access, salaries, among others.

Geological Province. An area with consistently related geological and genetic characteristics and dates from the same geological event. Such areas assist oil companies in determining which techniques to use when exploring for and producing oil whether in onshore or offshore areas.

Geophysical Surveys. These are means of studying a specific onshore or offshore area to ascertain whether oil and gas are likely to be found in the underlying rock.

Granting Clause. Clause contained in an oil and gas lease specifying the rights and interests granted by a lessor to a lessee.

Gravity. The measure of oil density used for price determination. It is also applicable to the weightiness of liquids, expressed in degrees with lower numbers indicating heavier liquids and higher numbers representing lighter liquids. Gravity is adopted by the American Petroleum Institute for measuring the density of liquid.

Grassroot Refinery. This is a new refinery built from scratch from conception to completion characterized by modern process and energy conservation technology. It is different from expansion of an existing refinery plant.

Greenfield. A new field with production prospects. Indeed, any project that is being developed from afresh. For example, an LNG plant being built from scratch.

Greenhouse Gases. Gases that alter thermal properties of atmosphere like water vapour, carbon dioxide, methane, nitrous oxide, halons and ozone that are transparent to solar (short-wave) radiation but opaque to long-wave (infrared) radiation, thus preventing long-wave radiant energy from leaving the earth's atmosphere.

Greenhouse Effect. The result of water vapour, carbon dioxide, and other atmospheric gases trapping radiant energy (absorbed radiation), thereby keeping the earth's surface warmer than it would otherwise be.

Gross Domestic Product (GDP). The total value of goods and services produced by labour and property within a particular country.

Gross Gas Withdrawal. The full-volume of compounds extracted at the wellhead, including nonhydrocarbon gases and natural gas plant liquids.

Gross Inputs. The crude oil, unfinished oils, and natural gas plant liquids put into atmospheric crude oil distillation units.

Gross National Product (GNP). This is the total market value of goods and services produced by a nation before deduction of depreciation charges and other allowances for capital consumption. GNP which is also widely used as a measure of economic activity includes the total purchases of goods and services by private consumers and government, gross private domestic capital investment, and net foreign trade.

Gross Production. The total volume of gas produced, including reproduced gas lift or injected gas.

Gross Withdrawals. The full well stream volume, including all natural gas plant liquid and nonhydrocarbon gases, but excluding lease condensate. It also includes amounts delivered as royalty payments or consumed in field operations.

Gross Value. Total value of hydrocarbon before tax deduction.

Halons. Halogenated carbon compounds used in fire extinguishing equipment and contributing to stratospheric ozone depletion. The Montreal Protocol endorsed its riddance.

Heating Fuels. This refers to any liquid, solid or gaseous fuel used for indoor space heating.

Heating Fuel Units. Standardized volumes for heating fuels.

Heavy Gas Oil. Petroleum distillates with an approximate boiling range from 651 degrees to 1000 degrees Fahrenheit.

Heavy Oil. The left-over fuel oils after the distillation of the lighter oils during the refining process. All petroleum used in steam plants is heavy oil, except for start-up and flame stabilization.

Held By Production (HBP). An oil and gas property which remains under lease beyond the primary lease term to the extent there is production in "commercial" quantities from the property.

Hexane. Petroleum liquid found in small amounts in condensates.

Horizon. A zone of a particular formation, such as the reservoir horizon possessing sufficient porosity and permeability to form a petroleum reservoir.

Horizontal Well. Used when reservoir permeability is low.

Horizontal Drilling. A flat level form of drilling technique, as against the normal vertical direction pattern of drilling.

Host Community. The community where crude oil is produced.

Host Government. The government of a foreign country where crude oil is produced.

Hot Tapping. A person or company linking or connecting its pipe to another's facilities in order to siphon or draw off crude oil illegally.

Hub. A location where several pipelines interconnect.

Hydrocarbon. An organic chemical compound constituted entirely by hydrogen and carbon. It may be in solid, liquid or gaseous form like coal, crude oil and natural gas respectively.

Hydrocracking. High pressure version of catalytic cracking in the presence of hydrogen.

Hydrogen. A colourless, odourless, and highly flammable gaseous element. It is the lightest of all gases which occurs together with oxygen in water as well as in acids, bases, alcohols, petroleum and other hydrocarbons.

Hydrogenation. Reacting coal with hydrogen at high pressures, usually in presence of a catalyst.

Hydrophone. Acoustical sensor used for collecting reflected waves in seismic exploration at sea.

Incident. An unplanned event or chain of events which has or could have caused injury or illness and/or damage or loss to environment, third parties or assets.

Injection Gas. Gas injected in gas-lift operations or a high-pressure gas injected into a formation to maintain or restore reservoir pressure.

Injection Water. Water pumped into a reservoir that helps drive hydrocarbons to a producing well .

Injector Head. This is a control head for injecting coiled tubing into a well that seals off the tubing and makes a pressure tight connection.

Injury. Physical harm or damage to a person resulting from traumatic contact between body of person and an outside agency, or from exposure to environmental factors.

Injury Frequency. Number of injuries per million man hours worked.

Injury Rate. Number of injuries per one hundred employees.

Injury Severity Rate. Number of days lost per one million man hours worked.

Instrumentation. These are devices used to measure, record and control a flow process in the petroleum industries. Instrumentation is made up of transmitters, controllers, sensor elements, and so on.

Jacket. The supporting lower part of an offshore platform. The section which is mainly in form of steel structure is positioned on the seabed with a deck to support drilling activities.

Jet Cutoff. A process for separating pipe stuck in a well through blast of special shaped-charge explosives similar to those used in jet perforating. The explosive is lowered into the pipe to the desired depth and detonated. The force of the explosion makes radiating horizontal cuts around the pipe, and the severed portion of the pipe is retrieved.

Jet Fuel. Aviation fuel also known as white product used for aircraft and obtained by distillation and sweetening.

Joint of Pipe. Various lengths or length of drill pipe or casing.

Joint Operating Agreement. An agreement regulating the operations of a jointly-owned facilities.

Joint Venture. Partnership involving two or more companies for the purposes of pooling resources together for the exploration and production of oil and gas activities.

Keep Whole. A clause in a gas agreement which allows the producer to receive an equivalent of the proceeds he would have been entitled to if he had sold the gas at the wellhead without processing.

Kelly Bushing. Drilling rig equipment that fits inside the rotary table and is also used as a reference point on logs to calculate depth.

Kelly Bypass. It is system of valves and piping that allows drilling fluid to be circulated without the use of the kelly.

Kerosene. This is a colourless and light petroleum distillate with low-sulfur content which burns without the emission of smoke. It is produced from the refining of crude oil with a boiling range at atmospheric pressure from 400 degrees to 550 degrees Fahrenheit.

Kick. When the formation pressure in an oil well exceeds the pressure exerted by the mud column.

Kick Fluids. This pertains to oil, gas, water, or any combination that enters the borehole from a permeable formation.

Kick-Off Well. A well whose inclination or orientation are determined to reach an area not directly below the well.

Kill. To control a kick by taking suitable preventive measures during drilling. During production, it means stopping a well from producing oil and gas so that reconditioning of the well can proceed.

Killing a Well. The use of drilling mud to fill a bore to stop the flow of oil or gas.

Kyoto Protocol. The outcome of negotiations at the third Conference of the Parties held in Kyoto, Japan in December 1977 where binding greenhouse gas emissions targets were set for countries that sign and ratify the agreement. The Kyoto Protocol covers methane, carbon dioxide, nitrous oxide sulfur hexafluoride, hydrofluorocarbons (HFCs) and perfluorocarons (PFCs).

Landfill Gas. Gas that is derived from the decomposition of organic material at landfill disposal sites. It contains approximately 50 percent methane.

Landed Cost. The cumulative price of imported fuel or crude oil at the port of discharge, including payments to producing countries and all transportation costs up to that point.

Landman. A company's focal point responsible for negotiating oil and gas lease agrements with other companies and other mineral owners.

Land Reclamation. The restoration or remediation of an area or portion of land from which resources have been recovered, to its original state. This may entail replanting of the land with new vegetation.

Land Take. Land expropriated by oil companies for the construction of oil facilities for the production of oil.

Lay Barge. A barge specifically equipped to lay submarine pipelines.

Leaded Gasoline. Fuel or petrol that contains more than 0.05 gram of lead per gallon.

Lead Time. The time it takes to complete a project, beginning from planning to completion stage.

Lease. A legal instrument, conveying the right to explore, drill and produce minerals resources including oil and gas from a portion of land for a specified period of time.

Lease and Plant Fuel. Fuel or natural gas used in lease operations for drilling, heaters, dehydrators and field compressors as well as in natural gas processing plants.

Lease Condensate. A mixture consisting primarily of pentanes and heavier hydrocarbons, recovered as a liquid from natural gas in lease separation facilities exclusive of butane and propane which are recovered downstream natural gas processing plants.

Lease Fuel. Natural gas used in well, field, and lease operations for drilling, heaters, dehydrators, and field compressors.

Lease Interests. Legal rights defined in an oil and gas agreement. This may be a lease between landowner and a company or independent operator.

Lease Operations. This refers to a well or lease or field operations relating to the exploration or production of natural gas prior to transmission out of the field for processing.

Lease Separation Facility. A facility used for separating gases from produced crude oil and water under temperature and pressure conditions as set by the separator.

Leasehold Reserves. Natural gas liquid reserves which correspond to the leasehold production.

Legatee. Person mentioned in a will and entitled to receive real or personal property as specified in the will.

Lessee. A person receiving a lease.

Lessor. A person who gives a lease.

Lessor's Royalty. Accrued share of gross production of minerals exclusive of cost of production, resulting from an oil and gas lease.

Lifting Costs. Cost associated with the extraction of minerals from a producing field.

Light Oil. Lighter fuel oils resulting from distillation during refining process. Light oils include kerosene, jet fuel and all petroleum used in internal combustion and gas-turbine engines.

Line-Miles of Seismic Exploration. The distance or length covered by seismic surveying on the Earth's surface.

Liner. Small diameter casing extending into producing layer from just inside bottom of final string of casing cemented in a well.

Liquefaction. This involves the process of producing liquid fuel from coal or the conversion of biomass from solid to liquid. It also means the process for making large amount of gasoline and heating oil from petroleum. The conversion process is made under an elevated temperatures and pressures.

Liquefied Gases. This is the liquid form of gases, some of which include butane, butylenes, ethane, ethylene, propane and propylene.

Liquefied Natural Gas (LNG). Natural gas that has been cooled under high pressure and converted into liquid form, shrinking substantially in volume for ease of transportation by ship. This is regasified upon delivery for distribution to end-users through pipeline.

Liquefied Petroleum Gas (LPG). It is a by-product of petroleum refining and derivative of natural gas production. It is constituted by a mixture of gaseous hydrocarbons, mainly propane and butane which transforms into liquid form under moderate pressure. It is used mainly as fuel for domestic purpose like in residential homes. Propane and butane may be used as mixtures or separately.

Loading Flange. Facilities used for delivering crude oil to a refinery.

Local Content or Nigerian Content. A policy which requires the multinational oil companies operating in Nigeria to utilize the human and material resources and services available in the country in the exploration, development, exploitation, transportation and sale of crude oil and gas resources derived from Nigeria. While it is the intention of government to boost the Nigerian economy through this process by the additional quantum of composite value to be derived, it also enjoined them to ensure that quality, health, safety and environmental standards are not compromised.

Local Distribution Company. A legal entity engaged in the distribution of natural gas through pipelines to consumers, namely, industrial, residential, commercial and transportation end-users.

Location Damages. Compensation paid by an operator to a land owner for actual and potential damages made to crops and economic trees during the course of drilling and operation of a well.

Log. The conduct of survey on a formation and interpretation of the results for information about the location of oil, gas and water.

Lost Time Injury (LTI). Work related injury or illness which prevents a person from further performing any work after the accident.

Lost Time Injury Frequency. Number of LTIs recorded for a group of workers, per million hours worked by that group.

Low Btu Gas. Fuel gas with a heating value ranging between 90 and 200 Btu per cubic foot.

Low-Sulfur Oil. Oil containing one percent or less of sulfur by weight.

Low Temperature Extraction Unit. Condensation of gas into a liquid by a process of refrigeration.

Lubes. Denser refined products like motor oil, grease or machine oil.

Lubricating Oils. Fluids used for reducing frictional parts.

Mains. A large pipe that transports large volume of gas from where smaller pipes are connected to supply consumers.

Major. A term which traditionally refers to the "Seven Sisters", namely, British Petroleum, Exxon, Gulf, Mobil, Shell, Chevron and Texaco, being the largest six oil producing companies in the world.

Major Natural Gas Producer. This refers to a person or entity who produces natural gas in substantial quantity large enough to have a major effect on energy supplies.

Major Marketer. Any person or entity who sells or trades in substantial volume of gas or oil large enough to have a major effect on energy supplies.

Major Oil Producer. Any person or entity who produces oil in substantial quantity, large enough to have a major effect on energy supplies.

Make-Up Gas. Gas which has been paid for previously under a take-or-pay clause in a gas purchase contract, but which is taken in succeeding years. The contract will normally specify the number of years after payment in which the purchaser can take delivery of make-up gas without paying a second time.

Make-Up Gas Period. The time period when an underproduced owner is making up the underproduced volumes of gas accumulated during a previous time period in which no gas was taken by taking his share of the gas, plus a percentage of the overproduced owners' gas, until the overproduced volumes are eliminated.

Mantle. Impermeable stratum overlaying a reservoir which prevents the hydrocarbons contained therein from migrating to other rocks.

Manufactured Gas. Gas derived through destructive distillation of coal or through decomposition of oil or through the reaction of steam passing through a bed of heated coal or coke. Blast furnace gas, coke oven gases, blue (water) gas, producer gas and coal gases are examples of manufactured gas.

Marine Riser. A pipe that connects offshore installation to a subsea wellhead for the purpose of drilling or production.

Market-Based Price. A price that is mutually agreed by several buyers and sellers in a competitive market.

Marginal Cost. The cost of producing one additional unit of a product.

Marginal Probability of Hydrocarbons (MPHC). The use of existing recovery technology based on current economic conditions to determine the probability of occurrence of oil and gas in commercial quantities.

Marginal Well. A well nearing maturity, whose natural resource is depleting to the extent that it becomes doubtful as to the viability of continued production.

Market Clearance Price. The price at which supply and demand are equal.

Marketing Costs. Costs incurred in making gas merchantable such as compression, dehydration, treating, and cost of transporting gas to the point of delivery to the purchaser.

Market-Out Provision. A provision in a gas contract which gives the purchaser the right to disconnect a well, if in the purchaser's opinion, the production of gas was uneconomical owing to well or market conditions.

Market Participant. Any person or entity who participates in the energy market either by way of selling, transmission or distribution of energy or ancillary services.

Marsh Gas. This is a colourless and odourless form of gas that bubbles to the surface of water in a swampy or marshy terrain. It can be explosive.

Master-Metering. Measurement of collective natural gas consumption of several tenants or housing units with a single meter.

Material Safety Data Sheet. This is issued by a manufacturer of chemical substances that sets out hazards likely to be encountered by those who come into contact with substance.

Maximum Efficient Rate (MER). The highest rate at which oil can be produced from an underground reservoir without damaging the reservoir or causing loss of reservoir pressure, capable of reducing the total amount of oil that may be recovered.

Mercaptan. An organic chemical compound with a sulfur- like odour (rotten eggs smell) that is added to natural gas before distribution aimed at serving as a safety device for detecting leakages.

Methane. A colourless, odourless and tasteless major constituent of natural gas representing the simplest of hydrocarbons. Pure methane is characterized by a heating value of 1,1012 Btu per standard cubic foot. It is formed by the anaerobic decomposition of organic matter, enteric fermentation in animals and is one of the greenhouse gases. It is used as a fuel and for manufacturing chemicals and it is highly inflammable.

Metric Ton. A standard measurement in the oil industry used extensively in place of barrels. A metric ton averages 7.5 barrels of crude oil and equivalent of 1,000 kilos.

Midstream. A term used to describe oil activities that fall between Upstream (exploration and production) and Downstream (refining and marketing), applicable mainly to the transportation of crude oil and natural gas.

Mineral. Naturally occurring homogeneous substance obtained from below the surface of the earth, namely, natural gas, sulfur coal, salt, sand, and petroleum.

Module. Self-contained box or package built with a specific purpose located on production installations.

Monopoly. A single seller with control over purchases of a specific market product.

Monopsony. A single buyer with control over purchases of a specific market product.

Multilateral Well. More than one horizontal section drilled in one well. Used to maximize number of wells that can be drilled from small installations.

Multiple Completion. The completion of a single well into more than one producing horizon, capable of producing simultaneously from the different horizons, or alternatively from each.

Naphta. A light oil distillate characterized by low molecular weight of hydrocarbons.

Natural Gas. A mixture of hydrocarbon gases containing high percentage of methane and varying amounts of ethane, butane, propane and other gases obtained from the earth. It is found in association with petroleum and coal deposits.

Natural Gas Field Facility. A gas field facility designed to process propane, butane, pentanes, etc. from natural gas as well control the quality of natural gas set aside for marketing. It is also designed to process natural gas produced from various fields for purposes of recovering condensate from a stream of natural gas.

Natural Gas Liquids (NGL). Hydrocarbon liquids found with and extracted from natural gas through the process of absorption, condensation, adsorption, or other methods in gas processing or cycling plants. Also, the portions of gas from a reservoir that are liquefied at the surface in field facilities or gas processing plants. NGL produced from gas processing plants are also known as liquefied petroleum gas (LPG).

Natural Gas Processing Plant. Facilities designed to process natural gas to recover natural gas liquids from a stream of natural gas that may or may not have passed through field separation facilities which controls the quality to be marketed.

Natural Gasoline. It refers to the mixture of liquid hydrocarbons (mostly pentanes and heavier hydrocarbons) extracted from natural gas, including isopentane.

Natural Gas Vehicle (NGV). Vehicles that are propelled or powered by natural gas that is compressed or liquefied.

Natural Gasoline. This is a mixture of liquids derived from natural gas.

Natural Reservoir Pressure. Energy which forces oil or gas to rise to the earth's surface when the reservoir is penetrated by an oil or gas well.

Near Miss Accident. An event capable of causing injury or damage but which was avoided or missed by circumstances.

Netback Purchase. Refers to a crude oil purchase agreement where the price paid for the crude is determined by sales prices of derivable products from the crude as well as other factors like transportation and processing costs.

New Field Discoveries. The volume of proved reserves of crude oil or natural gas discovered in a new field.

Non-Associated Gas. Natural gas produced from a productive reservoir with insignificant quantities of crude oil.

Non-Branded Product. Any refined petroleum product that is not branded.

Non-Dedicated (Non-contracted) Owner. Any person with interest in an oil or gas well but does not have a gas contract for his share of gas production and has neither not entered into any other agreement that governs the taking or sharing of gas.

Non-Dedicated Vehicle. A motor vehicle that can operate on alternative fuel, either on diesel or petrol/gasoline.

Non-Executive Mineral Interest. An interest in oil and gas which lacks the right to participate in the execution of oil and gas leases, but have a right to a share in the bonus and delay rentals as well as royalty under existing or future leases.

Non-Fungible Product. A blend stock that cannot be shipped through an existing petroleum product distribution systems because of incompatibility problems. For example, transporting petrol or gasoline or ethanol blends through petroleum product distribution systems which usually contains water, could lead to contamination.

Non-Participating Royalty Owner. A person who owns a severed portion of a royalty interest but who does not execute leases, participate in bonus sharing or rentals, or possesses rights of exploration and production.

Non-Recoverable Usage. Production from a well which is burned in support facilities such as generators, boilers, etc.

Non-Producing Reservoir. Reservoir in which oil or gas proved reserves have been identified but unable to produce despite deployment of gathering and transportation facilities.

Non-Renewable Fuels: Fuels like oil, natural gas and coal that cannot be easily made or renewed.

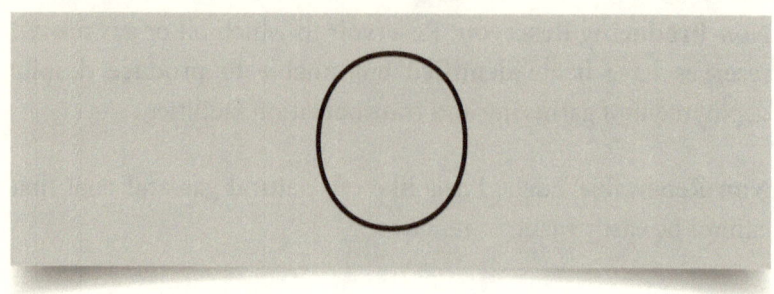

Octane. A flammable liquid hydrocarbon in petroleum used for measuring anti-knock properties in motor fuel. **Octane Rating.** The number used for indicating anti-

knock performance in motor vehicle engines or a measure of a gasoline or petrol's ability to burn without abnormal "knocking."

Odorant. Substance (mostly mercaptan) added to odourless natural gas to cause smell (mostly like rotten- egg) for purposes of detection during leakage.

Off Peak Gas. Gas that is scheduled for delivery on demand at a time demand is not at its peak.

Offset Royalty. Payment made in lieu of drilling an offset well and it is usually in accordance with the terms of agreed lease.

Offset Well. A well drilled on one tract of land aimed at preventing drainage of oil or gas from flowing to an adjoining tract of land on which there is an existing well that is being drilled or already in production.

Offshore. Geographical area that lies seaward of a coastline where oil fields and other facilities are located for the purpose of oil exploration.

Offshore Drilling. Drilling of wells beyond the shoreline to the high seas.

Offshore Oil Loading Nomenclature. Enables offshore loading with vessel swinging to present least resistance to prevailing wind or current conditions.

Off-System. Any point not on or directly interconnected with, a transportation, storage, and/or distribution system operated by a natural gas company. Put differently, where natural gas is transported to an end user by another (delivery) company other than by the company from whom the gas is purchased, namely, the producer or marketer.

Oil. A black mixture of liquid hydrocarbons of different molecular weights found beneath the earth. Gasoline or petrol and most plastics are made from oil.

Oil Field. A particular geographical area containing oil reservoir.

Oil in Place (OIP). An estimation of real amount of oil in a reservoir. Higher value than recoverable reserves of reservoir.

Oil Lost. Oil that is not retained in the production process for sale, and which has either spilled or burned.

Oil Payment. A share of oil or gas produced from a field or well exclusive of cost of production.

Oil Stocks. Available crude oil, natural gas plant liquids and refined petroleum products stocked for disposal.

Oil Reservoir. An underground pool of liquid consisting of hydrocarbons, sulfur, oxygen, and nitrogen trapped within a geological formation and protected from evaporation by the overlying mineral strata.

Oil Well. Any well with the capacity to produce one or more barrels of crude oil to each 100,000 cubic feet of natural gas.

On-System. A point directly interconnected with a transportation, storage, or distribution system operated by a natural gas company.

Onsystem (natural gas). Sale of natural gas by a local distribution company to an end user.

OPEC. An acronym for Organisation of Petroleum Exporting Countries (OPEC) established in 1960 to harmonise and coordinate petroleum industry policies of member-countries as well as negotiate with oil companies on matters of oil production, prices, and future concession rights. It has its headquarters in Vienna, Austria.

Operable Refineries. These are refineries that are either in operation or in bad shape but capable of being reactivated and brought back into full operation.

Operating Agreement. An agreement which specifies the basis of production, cost, ownership and operator's rights, powers and limits in a joint venture.

Operating Expenses. Incurred expenses arising from the operation of a producing field.

Operator (Gas Plant). A person responsible for the day-to- day management of a natural gas processing plant.

Operator (Oil/Gas Well). A person responsible for the day- to-day management of crude oil or natural gas wells.

Olefins. Basic chemicals made from oil or natural gas liquids feed stocks, used in the manufacture of plastics and gasoline or petrol, namely, ethylene and propylene.

Open Flow Test. An examination conducted to evaluate the volume of gas that can flow from a well within a particular timeframe with minimum restrictions.

Operator. A company or individual acting under an approved joint operating agreement, takes primary responsibility for day-to-day operations including drilling and the production of hydrocarbons on behalf of a consortium or joint venture.

Outer Continental Shelf. A term commonly used to refer to all submerged lands seaward and outside the area of lands beneath navigable waters.

Over-pressured Zone. An underground geological formation whose pressure exceeds normal levels.

Over-production. Output in excess of well's allowable ceiling.

Ozone. Allotropic form of oxygen having three atoms in each molecule, formula O3. Ozone formed in atmosphere from nitrogen oxides and organic gases emitted by automobiles and industrial sources.

Paid Up Lease. An oil and gas lease for which all delayed rentals are paid together with the cash bonus. Besides, no further action is required during the primary term

Participating Interest. The extent of ownership hold on a venture as expressed in percentage of costs and benefits accruable to investors under an Agreement.

Partnership. A contractual business relationship between two or more persons who have agreed to come together as co-owners of a joint venture for profit.

Payzone. Rock containing exploitable quantities of oil and gas.

Pentane. Lighter hydrocarbon like propane and butane. When these gases are mixed, could be liquefied and employed as fuels.

Permeability. Measurable capacity of rock to transmit fluid through pore spaces into wellbore.

Permit-To-Work. Written regulations aimed at controlling specific nature of work considered potentially hazardous.

Personal Protection Equipment. Protective equipment or clothing designed against risk to health and safety.

Petrochemical Feedstocks. Chemical feedstocks generated from petroleum basically for the manufacture of chemicals, synthetic rubber, and various types of plastics.

Petrochemicals. Chemicals derived from oil and manufactured as part of the refining process, namely, ethylene, propylene and benzene.

Petrolatum. Odourless, tasteless and greasy substance, obtained as residue from petroleum after lighter and more volatile components have been boiled off.

Petroleum. Generic name for hydrocarbons including crude oil, natural gas liquids, natural gas and their by- products that are still in their natural state beneath the earth.

Petroleum Products. Gasoline, kerosene, heavy fuel oil, lubricating oils, petroleum jelly, and paraffin consist principally of mixtures of paraffin hydrocarbons, which range from lighter liquid members to solid members. They are obtained from the processing of crude oil (including lease condensate), natural gas, and other hydrocarbon compounds.

Petroleum Refinery. A plant which manufactures finished petroleum products from crude oil, unfinished oils, natural gas liquids, other hydrocarbons, and alcohol.

Pig. Method for cleaning a pipeline or separating two liquids being transported through pipeline.

Piling. Long steel <u>piles</u> driven into seabed to solidly anchor fixed offshore structures.

Pipeline. This is hose-like metal used in conveying natural gas, crude oil or petroleum products between two points, either onshore or offshore. A pipeline is also used to convey gas through transmission from one point to its end user or ultimate consumer.

Pipeline Freight. This refers to freight carried through pipelines, including natural gas, crude oil, and other petroleum products.

Piping. It is an arrangement of pipes for the distribution and transportation of fluids to various locations.

Piping and Instrumentation Diagrams (P&ID). It is a diagram that shows the procedure and instrumentation behind the flow process of a system.

Pit. A hole in the ground used for temporary storage of fluids during drilling operations.

Planning Area. A subdivision of an offshore area used as the initial basis for considering blocs to be offered for lease.

Plant Condensate. One of the natural gas liquids, mostly pentanes and heavier hydrocarbons, recovered and separated as liquids at gas inlet separators or scrubbers in processing plants.

Plant Liquids. Those volumes of natural gas liquids recovered in natural gas processing plants.

Plant Products. Natural gas liquids recovered from gas processing plants as well as from field facilities. Products like ethane, propane, butane, butane-propane mixtures, etc.

Plateau. Level of peak oil or gas field production; it is always followed by declining level of production.

Platform. Facilities or fixed structure above sea level used for operating offshore fields.

Plugged and Abandoned Well. A depleted well where all the casings have been removed and the well bore sealed with mechanical or cement plugs and abandoned.

Plugging. The process whereby a well that is no longer needed is filled with concrete and abandoned.

Polymerisation. Refining process which uses low temperature reforming to increase the octane value of gasoline.

Pour Point. The ability of crude oil to flow at low temperatures.

Porosity. A characteristic of reservoir rock determined by its holes or spaces. Higher porosity rock can contain more hydrocarbons and is, therefore, considered a better quality of reservoir rock.

Possible Reserves. Reserves which cannot be classified as 'probable' but estimated to have significant but less than 50% chance of being technically and economically producible.

Prediscovery Costs. Costs incurred prior to discovery of minerals in commercially recoverable quantities in the extractive industry. This includes prospecting, acquisition, and exploration costs.

Preproduction Costs. Costs of prospecting for, acquiring, exploring, and developing mineral reserves incurred prior to the point when production of commercially recoverable quantities of minerals commences.

Primary Recovery. Recovery of oil or gas from a reservoir using only natural reservoir pressure. In other words, crude oil or natural gas recovered by any method that may be employed to produce them where the fluid enters the well bore by the action of natural reservoir pressure.

Primary Transportation. Conveyance of large shipments of petroleum raw materials and refined products usually by pipeline, barge, or ocean-going vessel. All crude oil transportation is primary, including the small amounts moved by truck. All refined product transportation by pipeline, barge, or ocean-going vessel is primary transportation.

Prime Supplier. A firm that produces, imports, or transports selected petroleum products across state boundaries and local marketing areas, and sells the product to local distributors, local retailers, or end users.

Probable Reserves. Those reserves which are not yet proven but which are estimated to have more than 50% chance of being technically and economically producible. Put differently, this refers to estimated quantities of energy sources that, on the basis of geologic evidence that supports projections from proved reserves, can reasonably be expected to exist and be recoverable under existing economic and operating conditions.

Process Fuel. Energy consumed in the course of acquisition, processing, and transportation of energy, particularly, relating to natural gas lease and plant operations, natural gas pipeline operations, and oil refinery operations.

Processed Gas. Natural gas that has gone through a processing plant for the extraction of liquefiable hydrocarbons.

Processing Gain. The volumetric amount by which total output is greater than input for a given period of time. This difference is due to the processing of crude oil into products which, in total, have a lower specific gravity than the crude oil processed.

Processing Loss. The volumetric amount by which total refinery output is less than input for a given period of time. This difference is due to the processing of crude oil into products which, in total, have a higher specific gravity than the crude oil processed.

Processing Plant. An installation designed to separate and recover natural gas liquids from a stream of produced natural gas through the processes of condensation, absorption, adsorption, refrigeration, or other methods and to control the quality of natural gas marketed and/or returned to oil or gas reservoirs for pressure maintenance, repressuring, or cycling.

Produced Water. Water that is extracted from the subsurface along with oil and gas, and may include water from the reservoir or water injected into the formation or any other chemicals added during the production/ treatment process.

Producer. Any party who owns, controls, manages, or leases any gas well. It also pertains to a company which engages in the production and sale of natural gas extracted from gas or oil wells.

Producible Lease. A lease where there has been hydrocarbon discovery in appreciable quantities, but for which there is no production during the reporting period.

Producible Zone Completion. The interval in a wellbore that has been mechanically prepared to produce oil, gas, or sulphur. There can be more than one zone completed for production in a wellbore.

Producing Lease. A lease that is producing oil, gas, or sulphur in quantities sufficient to generate royalties.

Product. This include residue from processed crude petroleum, refined crude oil, fuel oil, treated crude oil, natural gas, and other derivative of hydrocarbons.

Production. The phase of oil and gas operations involving well fluids extraction, separation, treatment, measurement, etc.

Production Capacity. The volume of product that can be produced from a processing plant.

Production Cost. This includes costs incurred while operating and maintaining wells and related equipment and facilities, including depreciation and applicable operating costs resulting from support equipment and facilities.

Production Drilling. Drilling of wells aimed at bringing a field into production.

Production Installation. An installation from which development wells are drilled.

Production Sharing Contract/Agreement. An arrangement between the host government and an oil producing company (also known as operator), which allows the operator to take the sole risk of exploration, development and production of an oil field. The operator takes all losses where oil is not found, but where otherwise, he recovers his costs, takes taxes, royalties and all other fiscal arrangement before sharing the profit between both parties in agreed ratio which also ensures the contractor earns a reasonable return on his capital investment.

Production String. Piping in a production well through which oil or gas flows from reservoir to wellhead.

Production Well. Well used when producing oil.

Propane. A hydrocarbon gas that is a constituent of crude oil or natural gas obtained through refining process from crude oil. It is used for industrial applications, lighting and heating. It is also a major component of liquefied petroleum gas (LPG) liquefied under pressure.

Proration. A system enforced by agreement between operators, limiting the amount of petroleum that can be produced from a well or a field within a given period.

Prospect. Underground area in which geologists believe there is possibility of finding oil.

Proven Field. An oil and/or gas field whose physical extent and estimated reserves have been determined.

Proven Reserves. Those reserves which on the available evidence are virtually certain to be technically and economically producible (i.e. having a better than 90% chance of being produced).

Pugh Clause. A clause in an oil and gas lease that releases non-producing acreage or zones at the end of the primary term or some other specified period. Under the clause, unproductive or untested zones and acreage that are outside a producing pooled unit must be released if drilling or exploration does not occur by the end of the specified time.

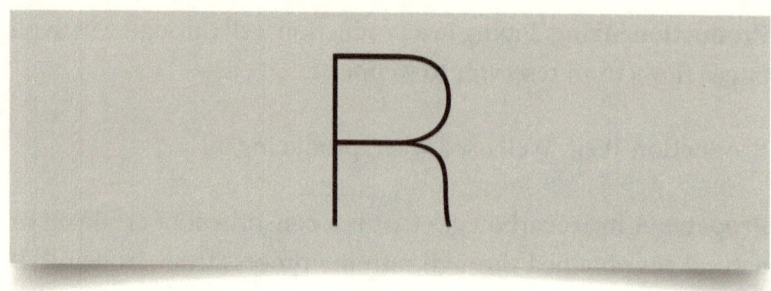

Rack Sales. Wholesale truckload sales or smaller of gasoline where title transfers at a terminal.

Rate Features. Special rate schedules or tariffs offered to customers by electric and/or natural gas utilities.

Reburn. An advanced co-firing technique using natural gas to reduce pollution from electric power plants.

Received. Gas and other petroleum products physically transferred into the responding company's transportation, storage, and/or distribution facilities.

Reclamation. The process of restoring surface environment to acceptable pre-existing conditions through surface contouring, equipment removal, well plugging, re-vegetation, etc.

Recompletion. After the initial completion of a well, the action and techniques of reentering the well and redoing or repairing the original completion to restore the well's productivity.

Recompletion Gas. Natural gas that is produced from a reservoir using well facilities that previously tapped a different, formerly non-productive reservoir.

Recoverable Proved Reserves. The proved reserves of natural gas of any given year. These are the estimated quantities of natural gas which geological and engineering data demonstrates with reasonable certainty to be recoverable in the future from known natural oil and gas reservoirs.

Recovery Factor. Ratio of recoverable oil and/or gas to estimated oil and/or gas in place in reservoir.

Redetermination. Retroactive adjustment to relative percentage interests of joint venturers in a field.

Re-Entry. Testing a potential zone by using the borehole of a plugged and abandoned well, usually after new drilling and production has occurred in the area.

Reference Month. The calendar month and year to which a reported cost, price, and volume information relates.

Reference Year. The calendar year to which a reported sales volume information relates.

Refined Petroleum Products. Refined petroleum products include but not limited to gasolines, kerosene, distillates, liquefied petroleum gas, asphalt, lubricating oils, diesel fuels, and residual fuels.

Refiner. A firm or the part of a firm that refines products or blends and substantially changes products, or refines liquid hydrocarbons from oil and gas field gases, or recovers liquefied petroleum gases incident to petroleum refining and sells those products to resellers, retailers or ultimate consumers.

Refinery. An installation that manufactures finished petroleum products from crude oil, unfinished oils, natural gas liquids, other hydrocarbons, and oxygenates.

Refinery Capacity Utilization. Ratio of the total amount of crude oil, unfinished oils, and natural gas plant liquids run through crude oil distillation units to the operable capacity of these units.

Refinery Fuel. Crude oil and petroleum products processed at the refinery for all purposes.

Refinery Gas. Non-condensate gas collected in petroleum refineries.

Refinery Losses and Gains. Processing gain and loss that takes place during the refining process itself, and it excludes losses that do not take place during the refining process, e.g., spills, fire losses, and contamination during blending, transportation, or storage.

Refinery Output. The total amount of petroleum products produced at a refinery, including petroleum consumed by the refinery.

Refinery Production. Petroleum products produced at a refinery or blending plant.

Refinery Utilization Rate. This represents the use of the atmospheric crude oil distillation units. The rate is calculated by dividing the gross input to these units by the operable refining capacity of the units.

Refinery Yield. This represents the per cent of finished product produced from input of crude oil and net input of unfinished oils. It is calculated by dividing the sum of crude oil and net unfinished input into the individual net production of finished products.

Reinjected. The forcing of gas under pressure into an oil reservoir in an attempt to increase recovery.

Reinserted Fuel. Irradiated fuel that is discharged in one cycle and inserted in the same reactor during a subsequent refuelling. In a few cases, fuel discharged from one reactor has been used to fuel a different reactor.

Reperforation. The creation of holes in oil well tubing.

Repressuring. The injection of gas into oil or gas formations to effect greater ultimate recovery.

Reseller. A firm that is engaged in a trade or business that buys refined petroleum products and then sells them to a purchaser who is not the ultimate consumer of those refined products.

Reserve Additions. The estimated original, recoverable, saleable, and new proved reserves credited to new fields and new reservoirs. It refers to domestic in-the-ground natural gas reserve additions.

Reserves. Generally, the amount of oil or gas in a particular reservoir that is available for production.

Reserves Changes. Positive and negative revisions, extensions, new reservoir discoveries in old fields, and new field discoveries that occurred during the year.

Reserves Probable. Reserves not yet "proven", but are estimated to have a better than 50% chance of being technically and economically producible.

Reserves Proven. Reserves which on available evidence are virtually certain to be technically and economically producible.

Reserves Revisions. Changes to prior year-end proved reserves estimates, either positive or negative, resulting from new information other than an increase in proved acreage (extension).

Reservoir. A porous and permeable formation containing significant quantities of hydrocarbons. A reservoir is characterized by a single natural pressure system.

Reservoir Capacity. The present total developed capacity of a reservoir, excluding planned future development.

Reservoir Drive. Powered by difference in pressures within reservoir and well.

Reservoir Engineering Model. It is used for predicting reservoir behaviour during production to enable selection of most efficient method of recovery.

Reservoir Repressuring. The injection of a pressurized fluid like air, gas and water into oil and gas reservoir formations to effect greater ultimate recovery.

Residential Consumers. Consumers using gas for heating, air conditioning, cooking, water heating, and other residential uses in single and multi-family dwellings and apartments.

Residue Gas. Gas remaining after processing through a plant for the extraction of liquids. Natural gas from which natural gas processing plant liquids products and, in some cases, nonhydrocarbon components have been extracted.

Residuum. Residue from crude oil after distilling off all but the heaviest components, with a boiling range greater than 1,000 degrees Fahrenheit.

Right-Of-Way. The land and legal right to use and service the land along which a pipeline or transmission line passes or located.

Road Oil. Any heavy petroleum oil, including residual asphaltic oil used as a dust palliative and surface treatment on roads and highways.

Rotary Rig. A machine used for drilling wells that employs a rotating tube attached to a bit for boring holes through rock.

Rotary Table (Drilling Table). A turning device on derrick floor in which drill-string is held and rotated. **Roughneck.** These are hard-manual labourers involved in the drilling process on a rig. They are typically rough and uncouth.

Round Trip. Complete process of pulling out and running in drill-string.

Roustabout. An unskilled labourer used as help for general duties jobs, including general maintenance and cleaning in the oil industry, specifically in field locations.

Royalty. The share of the production or proceeds from an acreage reserved for the owners. A contractual arrangement providing a mineral interest that gives the owner a right to a fractional share of production or proceeds therefrom, that does not contain rights and obligations of operating a mineral property, and that is normally free and clear of exploration, developmental and operating costs, except production taxes.

Royalty Cost. A share of the profit or product reserved by the grantor of a mining lease, such as a royalty paid to a lessee.

Royalty Interest. An interest in a mineral property provided through a royalty contract.

Rule of Capture. The theory that oil and gas produced under a particular tract is owned by the royalty owners therein, even though it may be proved to be part of the oil or gas that migrated from adjoining lands.

Run Statement. A monthly summary of run tickets given by the purchaser or operator of crude oil detailing volume, gravity, price, and value of each run ticket.

Run Ticket. A document evidencing the amount, gravity, temperature, etc. of oil being delivered. This document is the basis of payment for the oil. The term "run" is often used to describe the delivery or sale of oil.

S

Salt Water Disposal Well. A well used for the purpose of injecting produced water back into the ground.

Sand. A geological term for a formation beneath the surface of the earth from which hydrocarbons are produced. Its make-up is sufficientlyh homogeneous to differentiate it from other formations.

Sea Star. A semi-submersible type of oil rig used for depths of up to 3500 feet. The oil rig rests on hollow barges in a star configuration which is attached to the sea bed with tension legs that allow for a bit of movement due to rough weather.

Secondary Recovery. Hydrocarbons produced in one well bore by increasing reservoir pressure with water injected into an adjacent well bore. In other words, it is the recovery of oil and gas through the injection of liquids or gases into the reservoir, supplementing its natural energy. Secondary recovery methods are often applied when production slows due to depletion of the natural pressure.

Seismic Analysis. The seismic principle is to generate elastic waves methodically and study their propagation through the subsoil. The seismic waves are refracted and reflected as they travel through the various rock strata, and are detected at the ground or sea surface by appropriately placed geophones.

The seismic records are interpreted to generate information concerning the shape of the underground strata in the explored region.

Seismic Survey. Measurements of seismic-wave travel. Seismic exploration is divided into refraction and reflection surveys, depending on whether the predominant portion of the seismic waves' travel is horizontal or vertical. Refraction seismic surveys are used in exploration. Seismic reflection surveys detect boundaries between different kinds of rocks; this detection assists in mapping of geologic structures.

Self-Raising Platform: An offshore drilling platform fitted with large buoyancy tanks which are filled with seawater to keep the rig stable in the sea swell.

Separator. Apparatus that separates oil, gases, and water contained in the effluent at the exit from a production well, by making use of their respective densities. In other words, the separators operate based on the principle of gravity,

Separation. The process of separating liquid and gas hydrocarbons and water. This is typically accomplished in a pressure vessel at the surface, but newer technologies allow separation to occur in the wellbore under certain conditions.

Shale Shaker. Drilling mud passed over to sieve out cuttings.

Shutdown. A production hiatus during which the platform ceases to produce while essential maintenance work is undertaken.

Shut In. To close valves on a well to stop production. It also means a well on which the valves have been closed.

Shut-in Well. A well which is producing or capable of producing but is not produced, perhaps, due to non-availability of pipeline or market, among other factors.

Side-track. A well activity of drilling a new wellbore segment from a wellbore intersection to a new wellbore bottomhole or target.

Side-track Drilling. A remedial operation that results in creation of a new section of well bore for purpose of detouring around " junk", redrilling a lost hole or straightening crooked holes.

Slug Catcher. Plant installed in a gas pipeline system to catch unwanted "slugs" of liquid.

Solution Gas. Gas which is dissolved in oil in the reservoir under pressure.

Sounding Well. Hole for obtaining data concerning the characteristics of a field.

Sour Crude. Crude oil containing a substantial amount of sulphur, typically hydrogen sulphide. The sulphur content in sour crude is above 1 per cent.

Sour Gas. Any natural gas containing significant hydrogen sulphide.

Spacing. The distance between wells producing from the same reservoir, and it is based on what is deemed to be the amount of acreage that can be efficiently and economically drained by a well.

Spar Platform. A type of floating oil platform typically used in very deep waters, and is named for logs used as buoys in shipping that are moored in place vertically. Spar production platforms have been developed as an alternative to conventional platforms.

Split Stream Gas Well. The separate sales of gas by owners with interests in a well to two or more pipeline purchasers where there are two or more pipelines running to the well.

Spot Market. It is a short term, non-regulated, arms' length contract sales of natural gas, crude oil, refined products, or liquid petroleum gas. It is usually characterised by 30 days duration with provision in force until is specifically terminated by either party. Renewals are mainly based on new letters of agreement.

Spud. Commencement of drilling operations.

Spud Date. The date that drilling begins.

Spud-in. Operation of drilling the first part of a new well.

Stimulation. It refers to several processes to enlarge old channels, or create new ones, in the producing formation of a well designed to enhance production.

Storage Gas. A gas that is stored in an underground reservoir.

Storage Tank. Tank used for the accumulation of oil pending when it is dispensed to a purchaser or transferred to a pipeline.

Subsea Manifolds. This allows wells to be put on production without need to build a platform to operate and maintain wells.

Subsea Production Systems. These are typical wells located on the seabed, shallow or deep water. Generally termed as Floating production system, where the petroleum is extracted at the seabed and the same can be tied back to an already existing production platform or an onshore facility.

Subsea Wellhead. A wellhead installed on the sea floor and controlled remotely from a platform, a floating production facility or land.

Substandard Acreage. Amount of acreage that is less than the standard amount for a proration unit for a field.

Substructure. Support form of an offshore installation on which derrick, engines, helicopter pad, cranes, etc. are installed.

Sulphur Dioxide. Acts as a precursor in formation of sulphate aerosols which, unlike greenhouse gases, have a net negative radiative forcing effect and tend to cool Earth's surface.

Surface Casing. Outer casing cemented in the upper portion of the wellbore to protect fresh water formations from contamination.

Surface location. The location of a well or facility or measurement point.

Surface Reclamation. Restoration of surface to a productivity or useful level.

Suspended Discovery. An oil or gas field identified by a discovery well but not being produced or developed.

Suspended Well. A well that has been capped off temporarily.

Sweet Crude. Crude oil with low sulphur content.

Sweet Gas. All natural gas except sour gas and casing head gas. Specifically, sweet gas is a natural gas with little or no hydrogen sulfide.

Synfuels. Synthetically petroleum products produced from coal or natural gas.

Synthetic Natural Gas. Gases made from coals and other hydrocarbon-containing substances.

Tank Battery. Tanks for oil storage before delivery to a refinery.

Temporarily Abandoned. The act of isolating the completed interval or intervals within a wellbore from the surface by means of a cement retainer, cast iron bridge plug, cement plug, tubing and packer with tubing plug, or any combination thereof.

Tension Leg Platform. A floating offshore structure held in position by a number of tension-maintaining cables anchored to seabed. Cables dampen wave action to keep platform stationary.

Term Interest. Interest in royalty or mineral calculated upwards of 10 years, as against perpetuity.

Terminal. Plant and equipment designed to receive and process crude oil or gas to remove water and impurities. An onshore transit installation that receives oil or gas from offshore production facilities via pipeline and/or tankers.

Tertiary Recovery. Use of recovery methods that restore formation pressure as well as improve oil displacement or fluid flow in reservoir. It also connotes the application of any improved recovery method for the removal of additional oil.

Test Well. The first well to be drilled on a lease in order to evaluate a certain horizon. It is also known as "Wild Cat" well.

Three Dimensional Seismic (3-D). Advanced method for collecting, processing, and interpreting seismic data in three dimensions. 3-D data are collected from closely spaced lines over an area and the data are processed as a volume. It is used for determining best places to drill for hydrocarbons. Some of the advantages include increased resolution, improved interpretational tools and data displays.

Throughput. The total amount of raw materials processed by a refinery or other plant in a given period.

Tight Formation Gas. Gas produced from a sedimentary layer of rock cemented together in a way that obstructs the flow of any gas through the rock.

Tight Hole. A well whose formation is curtailed for security or competitive reasons.

Tight Sand. Sand or sandstone formation with low permeability.

Toolpusher. Second-in-command of a drilling crew under the drilling superintendent. Responsible for the day-to-day running of the rig and for ensuring that all the necessary equipment is available.

Top Drive. Powerful electric motor that rotates whole drill- string from top down.

Topping. The primary distillation phase of a refinery process, and by derivation, the type of refinery and its yield of products. The topper heats crude oil at atmospheric pressure to accomplish the first rough distillation cut. The lighter products produced in this process are further refined in the catalyhtic cracking unit or the reforming unit. Heavier products which cannot be vaporized and separated in this process are distilled still further in the vacuum distillation unit or the coker.

Topsides. Top of an installation positioned on jacket, encompassing the surface deck of a platform, which includes all equipment for drilling, production and processing. The topside operation can include oil and gas treatment, storage and offloading, process support systems, as well as the living quarters for those that work on the rig.

Total Depth. The maximum depth reach in a well.

Traditional Gas Sales Contracts. This refers to a long term contract with numerous provisions such as price, deliverability, take-or pay, quality of gas, etc. made with a pipeline company.

Tray. Flat, perforated snelves at prescribed levels in a distillation tower, which allow specific vaporized crude oil components to pass through and then condense on their surfaces (after contacting domes called bubble caps above the perforations) before being drawn off for further distillation.

Treating. Removal of contaminants from gas by mechanical or chemical means.

Treating Plant. A plant designed to remove contaminants from natural gas.

Treatment. Set of procedures for separating the various components of the effiuent and obtaining crude oil.

Tubing. String of pipe set inside the well casing, through which the oil or gas is produced.

Turn-Around Maintenance. Scheduled large-scale maintenance activity of a process unit or plant.

Unbundling. This refers to the separation of sales and transport activities in the natural gas transmission and distribution sectors. Generally, it is applicable to the separation of various industry functions for purposes of billing and offer for services.

Unconventional Gas. Gas whose costs of production is higher than its current market value.

Underbalanced Drilling. Drilling under conditions where the pressure being exerted inside the wellbore is less than the pressure of the oil or gas in the formation.

Underground Hydrocarbon Storage. The use of sub-surface geologic formation for storing liquid, liquefied or gaseous hydrocarbons, such as natural gasoline, propane and natural gas.

Underground Injection. The placement of gases or fluids into an underground reservoir through a wellbore. It may be used as part of enhanced oil recovery or waterflooding processes or for disposal of produced water.

Underproduction. Production that is less than the allowable assigned to a proration unit.

Unloading a Well. The process of removing fluid from the tubing in a well, often by means of a swab, to lower the bottomhole pressure in the wellbore at the perforations and induce the well to flow.

Upstream. The process of exploring, developing and producing oil from oil fields.

Unitization. Joint operations to maximize recovery among separate operators within a common reservoir.

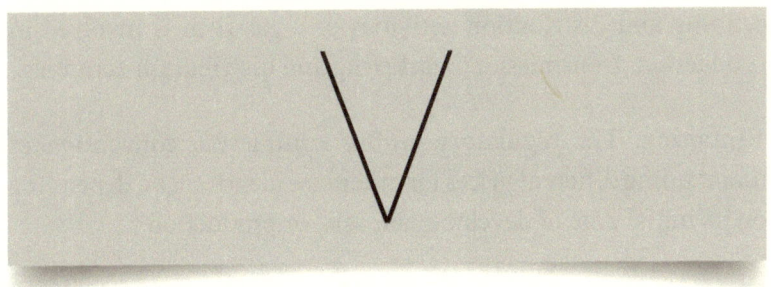

Vacuum Distillation. The process by which heavier cuts of crude not vaporized in the topping process are heated in a vacuum to accomplish their fractionation.

Value-Of-Service Pricing. A system of assigning costs among utility customers so that users who place a greater value on the service are charged higher rates than the more price-sensitive customers. For example, for natural gas pipelines, the largest element in variable costs is the cost of compressor fuel.

Variable Cost. The portion of a utility's cost of service which varies with the volume of sales.

Vent. Gas safety exhausting system to avoid dangerous excess pressures building up.

Venting. Release of gases to atmosphere.

Vertical Integration. When a company is involved in more than one commercially separable industrial function. For example, when an oil firm participates in production, refining and distribution activities or a gas firm is involved in production, transmission, marketing and distribution activities.

Vintaging. The regulatory and/or contractual convention of maintaining different prices for otherwise identical gas, depending on its initial date of development, sale, or production.

Visbreaking. A thermal cracking process applicable to residue of vacuum distillation as part of the overall conversion process.

Viscosity. The ability of a liquid to flow at a given

Volatility. The ability of a liquid to evaporate.

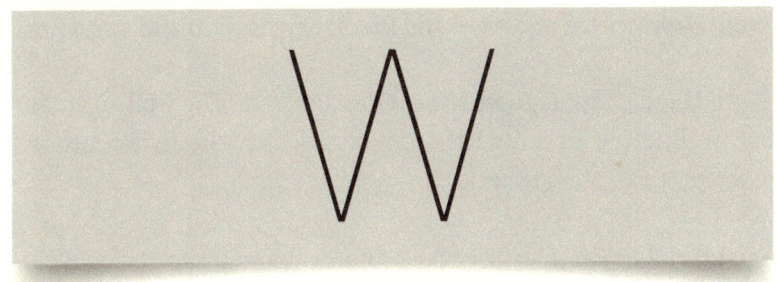

Warranty Clause. The clause in an oil and gas lease that confers title to the leased property by an express covenant to that effect.

Warranty Contracts. Gas contracts in which a producer commits to deliver a volume of gas with no specification as to the field of origin and with none of the production-related caveats that are commonly attached to contracts backed by dedication of gas from specific acreage, reservoirs, or wells.

Waterflooding. The injection of water into an oil reservoir to push additional oil out of the reservoir rock and into the wellbores of producing wells.

Water Injection. Water is pumped into alternate wells in a field. Pressure in reservoir as a whole can be maintained or increased and production can be maintained or increased.

Wellbore. This refers to a hole made by drill bit for oil or gas production on a completed well.

Well Completion. The process by which a finished well is either sealed off or prepared for production by fitting a wellhead.

Well. Hole drilled underground for oil exploration and operation.

Well Head. The equipment at the surface of a well used for controlling the pressure; the point at which the hydrocarbons and water exit the ground.

Well Head Price. The price paid for gas at a well site. It also mean the price or value in the first sale of oil or gas, for regulatory, royalty or tax purposes.

Well Jacket. A protective structure built around an offshore well to keep vessels or floating debris from damaging wellhead.

Well Log. A record of geological formation penetrated during drilling, including technical details of the operation.

Well Servicing. Maintenance work performed on an oil or gas well to improve or maintain the production.

Wet Gas. Natural gas containing significant amounts of liquefiable hydrocarbons.

White Oil. The lightest products resulting from the refining process as distinct from black oil.

Wildcat Well. A well drilled in an area where no current oil or gas production exists. Put differently, it is a well drilled in an unproven area aimed at discovering a new field or reservoir. The term came from West Texas, where in early 1920s drilling crews encountered many wildcats as they cleared locations for exploratory wells. Shot wildcats were hung on oil derricks, and wells became known as wildcat wells.

Workover. The performance of one or more of a variety of remedial operations like deepening, plugging back, pulling resetting liners, etc. on a producing oil well aimed at restoring or increasing production. It is a remedial work to the equipment within a well, the well pipework, or relating to attempts to increase the rate of flow. A workover may be performed to stimulate the well, remove sand or wax from the wellbore, to mechanically repair the well, or for other reasons. It is a re-entry into a completed field well for modification or repair.

Wireline. Wire or cable used for downhole operations, for example lowering instruments into a well.

Zone. The way pipeline companies differentiate between different areas on their pipeline systems. Each pipeline system has a field zone and a market zone. Gas may be delivered into the pipeline's field zone (usually) and taken out of the system in market zones.

Zone Rate. A transportation service rate whereby costs for transportation will be set based upon the zone or number of zones through which gas travels under a particular transaction.

Zone Tariff. This refers to the transmission rates that vary between geographic units but are uniform within any single unit.

END-NOTES

1. U. S. Energy Information Administration (Independent Statistics and Analysis)
2. Wikipedia, The Free Encyclopaedia
3. E & P Consultancy Associates
4. Mbendi Information Services

www.ingramcontent.com/pod-product-compliance
Lightning Source LLC
Chambersburg PA
CBHW022007170526
45157CB00003B/1185